Lillian Too

Creating abundance with feng shui

*'You shall decree abundance for yourself
and it shall be established for you . . .
An open mind and a gentle heart,
a determination to enrich your life.
And feng shui will astonish you
with truly marvellous results.'*

RIDER

London • Sydney • Auckland • Johannesburg

First published in 1999

3 5 7 9 10 8 6 4

First published in 1999 by Rider,
an imprint of Ebury Press
Random House, 20 Vauxhall Bridge Road, London SW1V 2SA
www.randomhouse.co.uk

Random House Australia (Pty) Limited
20 Alfred Street, Milsons Point, Sydney,
New South Wales 2061, Australia

Random House New Zealand Limited
18 Poland Road, Glenfield,
Auckland 10, New Zealand

Random House South Africa (Pty) Limited
Endulini, 5a Jubilee Road,
Parktown 2193, South Africa

The Random House Group Limited Reg. No. 954009

Papers used by Rider are natural, recyclable products made from wood
grown in sustainable forests

Printed in Great Britain by Butler & Tanner Ltd, Frome and London

A CIP catalogue record for this book is available from the British Library

ISBN 0-7126-7036-X

To Jennifer,
Now more than ever.

Contents

Foreword

CREATING ABUNDANCE is more than just making money. Abundance embraces all the wonderful things that deepen and expand one's life. There are eight types of abundance which make life meaningful – the abundance of material possessions, of recognition, of success, good health, loving relationships, good family life, meaningful personal growth and the simple phenomena of feeling good about yourself. I call this the feel good wealth, and it describes the generous and good heart that is the best outcome of possessing abundance. This is the situation of ultimate happiness because it engages the spiritual high side that is latent inside all of us.

There are different ways of creating abundance. My way combines the development of a strong yet relaxed sense of personal determination combined with the clever use and application of feng shui. Feng shui is an ancient Chinese cultural practice that advocates living in harmony with the environment. It prescribes methods for creating harmony in your living space, enabling you to move in tune to the patterns and vibrations of the energy around you. The result is a melodious blending of personal vitality with that of the environment. And this, in turn, creates an overflow of auspicious cosmic chi. It is this chi that attracts abundance, wealth, prosperity, health, acclaim, popularity and happiness.

Feng shui is very easy to put into practice and elementary level feng shui works just as well as advanced feng shui. There are many things that are splendid about the practice of feng shui, not least its fundamental philosophy that life is a dynamic process of change. This tenet comes from the inspiring wisdom of the *I Ching* – The Book of Changes.

The central theme of the *I Ching* is that the Universe is in a continuous state of flux, constantly evolving and changing. Good fortune transforms into misfortune that likewise transforms into good fortune. Our situation in life is never static. Just when we believe that all is lost, something – or someone – comes along with a solution, thereby easing our material discomforts, our illness or our despair.

And just when we become complacent and arrogant about our success, overnight we can find our world shattered and in pieces. Feng shui makes life easier when our luck turns bad and it brings stunning success when our luck turns good. It enhances the highs and reduces the lows. Feng shui creates arrangements and orientations that improve the energies of the surrounding space thereby attracting great good fortune in good times, and dissolving ill fortunes in bad times.

But feng shui also works in tandem with the spiritual strength and generosity of spirit that is inherent in mankind. Feng shui is the luck of the earth, and it brings opportunities for a better material life. To optimize earth luck, it has to be combined with mankind luck, the luck we create for ourselves before any seed of good fortune can take root and grow into harvestable good fortune.

The more you can combine this material abundance brought by earth luck with the spirituality, creativity and perseverance of mankind luck, the greater will be the abundance sustained. The practice of feng shui is thus multi-level and dynamic.

It requires sensitivity not only to the delicate changing energy patterns that are caused by alterations to physical landscapes, but also to the inherent energies of the self. Learning to tune into the energies of a changing landscape and a changing self, combines the best of feng shui practice with the power of the relaxed mind.

Changes in the energy patterns of landscapes and in the human psyche affect the feng shui of personal space. Both are also affected by the passage of time. Feng shui awareness helps you to acquire sensitivity to the quality and characteristics of the energies in the space around you. Feng shui knowledge enhances your ability to refine and improve these energies so they become auspicious, friendly and harmonious, thereby bringing good fortune.

This book reveals how you can make the surrounding energies work powerfully for you rather than against you. It also shows you how to strengthen and speed up the positive results of feng shui enhancements by combining feng shui practice with the use of your mind, your creativity and your imagination. In the process, you will find your life becoming increasingly surrounded by abundance, happiness and a sense of well-being.

Lillian Too

1 Programming for abundance

'You shall decree
Abundance for yourself
And it shall be established for you . . .
An open mind and a gentle heart,
A determination to enrich your life.
And feng shui will astonish you
With truly marvellous results.'

HOW BADLY do you want abundance in your life? How many times have you sat down to think about all the good things you want? How comfortable are you with wanting material prosperity, success, recognition, more money, more free time, an easier lifestyle, love, genuinely fulfilling relationships, popularity, great good health and lots and lots of success? In fact, all the aspirations you can think of that will make you happy and fulfilled.

You should start by thinking deeply about all the aspirations in your life. If you want success, you must identify what kind of success you want. If you want a relationship, you should likewise think through exactly the kind of relationship you want. Feng shui has the potential to enhance and actualize all your aspirations. Thinking them through will go a long way towards making this happen in exactly the way you want them to.

Until you have thought about abundance, and also feel comfortable about wanting it in your life, it will be difficult to attract the manifestations of abundance. Unless you know what you want with clarity and a relaxed determination, you will not get them. No matter what you do or which new method you try, it will not work. To successfully create abundance you must want it with a passion. You must imbue what you want with a single-minded focus. Only then can you empower your efforts and ensure they meet with success. There must be eagerness and enthusiasm. And it helps if you know exactly what type of abundance you want. The more you clarify the kind of luck you are working towards, the sharper and more effective will be the energies you can succeed in creating.

Be passionate about what you want. But let it be a relaxed passion. Guard against generating an obsessive attachment to a successful outcome. When you place too much pressure on getting what you want, tension is created, which generates a negative energy and this works against you.

It's OK *to be sceptical*

When you first hear about feng shui and initially read about the exciting promise of this ancient body of knowledge, it is perfectly understandable if you feel sceptical. When you are asked to believe that merely by living in harmony with your environment and in accordance with feng shui, you will be able to actualize all the success, prosperity and well-being that brings abundance into your life, you will surely be doubtful. You should accept that one possible reaction from deep within you to all this hype is a healthy dose of scepticism.

Feng shui does indeed work like magic, and there is often a seemingly mysterious force at work. So it is perfectly understandable to feel wary and be suspicious of all these claims. I felt exactly like that all those years ago when I first came across feng shui. And it took me a long time to take feng shui seriously.

That did not stop me from experimenting and as a result I benefited hugely. I reasoned that there was nothing to lose if all I needed to do was move my desk position, change my sleeping direction or place a water feature in my garden. I was convinced that the up-side to doing these simple things could well be phenomenal. I viewed feng shui with scepticism and amusement. Until it brought us our daughter.

My husband and I had been childless during the first ten years of our marriage, and it was with the help of feng shui that Jennifer came to us. In retrospect, and looking at the way our lives have been filled with such an abundance of happiness, prosperity and fulfilment, I believe that the initial decision to give feng shui a chance to work its special kind of dragon magic on our lives was a rather wise decision.

Of course, there had been no down-side to that decision. I had nothing to lose! Today I am convinced it was this attitude that made me benefit enormously from feng shui. Both my career and my personal life blossomed and in later years, when I activated my money luck by energizing a special wealth luck technique, I made more than enough money within 18 months to retire permanently from corporate working life!

Feng shui has also benefited me in a host of other ways, too numerous to go into all at once. Suffice to say that feng shui has also benefited my family as well. My husband and I enjoy the best of great good health. We have been together now for over 30 years. We have beautiful homes and a lovely lifestyle. Last year, Jennifer graduated from Cambridge and has now started working life. It is not, of course, all due to feng shui. But feng shui has helped in a meaningful and positive way.

Feng shui brings positive results when you practise it correctly. It will not work when you get it wrong. When applying recommendations, however, mistakes can be made at any stage of the process. Thus you could well have taken your directions incorrectly. Or you might have demarcated your personal space wrongly. Or you may have got your directions mixed up. Mistakes happen when you are too tense. Your practice of feng shui will work better if you maintain a serene attitude. Look on it with a relaxed conviction that you understand what you are doing and refrain from generating negative energy with excessive tension. The chances of feng shui working for you will then be incredibly enhanced. Results will come faster than you realize.

When you understand this fine point, you will be ready to use feng shui and apply its different techniques to attract all and every kind of abundance into your life. The key is to believe in yourself rather than in the practice of feng shui itself. In fact, when you have decided clearly how you wish to apply feng shui to improve and enhance your living space, it is more important to believe in yourself and have confidence that you are doing it right than to believe in feng shui.

The simplicity of practising feng shui

It is easy to be drawn to the simplicity of feng shui's practice and to be attracted to its underlying philosophy. Although the origins of feng shui go back three thousand years, its many guidelines on arranging the living space to attract harmonious and auspicious energies are extremely simple once you understand the basis upon which these guidelines are formulated.

The great Chinese classic, the *I Ching* has influenced the evolution of feng shui enormously, and this is why so many of feng shui's guidelines appear similar to other Chinese practices that are also based on the same philosophy of the *I Ching*. The essence of the *I Ching's* philosophy is that the luck of mankind is constantly changing and evolving, turning in immutable rhythms from good fortune to misfortune and back to good fortune again.

This cycle of good and bad luck can be strongly modified if you understand the secrets of the earth's energies and how to manipulate them. This is the science of feng shui which, when used correctly can modify periods of bad luck so that misfortunes are then made small. Feng shui can also enhance periods of good luck so that auspicious good fortune can be multiplied a hundred-fold!

It is tempting to speculate that the current popularity of feng shui is a passing fad, and to view it as frivolous fancy picked up from the Orient. But such a view suggests a lack of understanding of the practice of feng shui.

There is a great depth and breadth to its practice. Once you see this and realize its vast possibilities, feng shui will start to fascinate you. You will find it very easy to learn and practise. And when you also see how it fulfils the promise of its great potential, feng shui will not only become fun to practise, you will also become increasingly awed by it.

What exactly is feng shui?

Feng shui is a method and a technique. It is a specialized body of knowledge that can be regarded as both a science and an art. It is a science because the correct practice of feng shui requires very exact measurements of dimensions and compass directions. Indeed, the use of feng shui formulas is frequently so potent and works so fast when dimensions and measurements are correctly taken that those who benefit soon become ardent practitioners.

The Chinese of Hong Kong and Taiwan, for instance, will seldom change homes or offices without first consulting the feng shui man. My personal approach, however, tends to be more relaxed. I strongly believe that feng shui is something you can do by yourself. I do not advocate using a feng shui consultant for the home since this is both expensive and invasive. It is better to keep the privacy of one's home private by learning feng shui correctly and then enjoy slowly improving the feng shui of your home yourself.

Feng shui masters should, however, be used for corporate offices. Bringing in a professional consultant for business improvements to the work space works wonders for the bottom line. Feng shui is an art and correct diagnosis of what is wrong usually benefits from the experienced eye of the experienced master practitioner. Good judgement in feng shui, as in any other profession, calls for a background of experience. This is especially true of the branch of feng shui that is less scientific and relates to the determination of landscape types, the energies of contours, and the feng shui characteristics of elevations within the environment. This aspect of feng shui practice requires a well-trained eye, and a great deal of experience.

Feng shui requires both subjectivity and objectivity. It is a Chinese symbolic practice and, as such, it is tempting to dismiss it as superstition. But feng shui is embedded deep in the Chinese psyche and can correctly be regarded as a cultural and traditional custom. At the same time, there are similar practices in other countries that might well resemble feng shui but their fundamentals differ and although certain recommendations may be similar, the root rationales are not the same, often quite substantially – Vastu from India and dowsing to locate water ley lines are but two examples of practices that are similar to feng shui.

Keeping an open mind

If you want to use feng shui to enhance your life, it is advisable to keep an open mind. Delve into the secrets of feng shui. There is little cost to doing so as it is neither spiritual *per se* nor mysterious. It does not require you to compromise any of your religious faiths or principles because its practice does not call for any kind of worship, sacrifice or faith.

Instead, if you want to benefit from feng shui, you must accept that it is intrinsically alien to the Western mind. Feng shui uses a great deal of cultural symbolism to describe much of the rationale behind its tenets. The language of feng shui is tied up with ancient legends that speak of celestial creatures, auspicious plants, fruits, flowers, trees and other good fortune symbols.

The rationale behind many feng shui recommendations can often seem strange to the Western scientific tradition. There are extensive references to the yin and yang aspects of energy. It also presupposes an acceptance of the fundamental premise that the Universe and all that is in it is made up of one of five elements – earth, water, wood, metal and fire – which have a circular destructive and productive relationship to each other. Indeed, understanding the interactions of these five elements in the context of space and time dimensions make up a large part of the study of feng shui. These concepts are totally foreign to the Western concept of the Universe. Feng shui brings an entirely new perspective to how the environment is viewed.

Many of the old texts speak in indirect terms, often using the most metaphorical language to describe the methods and the outcome that can be expected. This can result in there being several interpretations to basic feng shui ideology that can differ from one practitioner to the next.

Feng shui can assail the senses and frustrate the new practitioner. So if you want to use feng shui to enhance your life, it may sometimes be necessary to suspend judgment and disbelief. Once the knowledge clicks into place, however, you will wonder how you could possibly ever have missed all the things that feng shui speaks about. This is because so much of feng shui is common sense once it has been pointed out to you. It's like knowledge lying dormant at the edge of your consciousness.

When you have done much reading; I advise you to also undertake some meditative thinking on the subject. Turn it over in your mind and explore the many layers of feng shui interpretations of the environment based on the different schools of thought. Most importantly, try to see what kind of results it brings into your life.

In time, as you become adept at it, feng shui takes your breath away! You will wonder how you ever lived without it.

How does feng shui work?

If you are reading about feng shui for the first time, you will be wondering how feng shui actually works. For example, you will read later on that I strongly recommend placing a tortoise in the north to attract enormous success and prosperity luck. To someone new to the practice of feng shui it will definitely require a leap of credibility to believe this. Similarly, by what special process could I possibly explain how, simply by placing the model of a three-legged toad in the home, your income and wealth will be enhanced? Or how does planting a bamboo grove in the garden lengthen the life of every resident of the house?

I have to confess that I am unable to explain exactly how feng shui works. But I can say that I have seen these simple symbolic enhancements of the living space create superb new luck for hitherto unhappy and unlucky families. However, I have found that much of successful feng shui practice has to do with attributes associated with the way good luck symbols are placed around the home. Feng shui actualizes the symbolism of the mind and very often, the clearer the mind grasps the symbolism, the more effective will all the energizers turn out to be. Once you begin to understand this aspect of feng shui, you will see just how effective feng shui can be when combined with the power of the mind.

Hence, while feng shui is the science of space, it is also a reflection of the mind. It actualizes on the physical and material plane all that the mind associates with the symbols that are used in the practice of feng shui.

When you keep your mind open and receptive to feng shui's many different methods for becoming rich and healthy, your own personal energies will start to help you formulate the way you should create your personal space. Then the flow of chi in your space will bring auspicious energies into your life.

Entering the world of feng shui

In recent years, a great deal of attention has been focused on alternative methods of healing and of dealing with stress and work pressure. Wonderful new methods that originate from various cultures around the world have opened new ways of diagnosing blockages that impede the flow of internal energies within the physical body. Growing acceptance of alternative phenomena has led to exciting breakthroughs in holistic healing methods.

The world of modern medicine has already acknowledged the wonderful curative powers of ayurvedic medicine from India and acupuncture techniques for easing pain from China. And increasingly we are beginning to discover the huge potential of aromatherapy. These alternative methods for improving the health of the human body have been gaining mainstream appeal and establishment acceptance because they have been shown to work.

Feng shui broadens the scope of the alternative phenomena still further except that its exciting promise encompasses the entire gamut of mankind's aspirations. Feng shui is not just for enhancing incomes and gaining success at work or in business. Rather, it holds the potential for a life filled with every kind of abundance – from great wealth and prosperity to the abundance of personal growth, from acclaim and recognition to success in any endeavour. Feng shui also offers the luck of good health and longevity, of love and relationships, and of a meaningful and happy family life.

It has the potential of fulfilling our wishes and aspirations on various levels, and when combined with the power of the fully awakened mind, there is no limit to the great good fortune it can bring to our lives.

The best way to combine the mind's vast potential to actualize dreams and aspirations is to study the various methods of feng shui and understand the symbolism contained in its guidelines. Then use the mind to strongly visualize the relevant feng shui enhancer or energizer working powerfully in the corner of the house, apartment or room in which it has been placed. Visualized feng shui is very potent. I use it all the time to reinforce what I have done to arrange the living space as harmoniously as possible. I have discovered that sending strong signals of positive energy to my personal space greatly enhances the good feng shui features that I have physically introduced.

Before using your powers of visualization to enhance your feng shui, however, it is necessary to understand its fundamental practice. Try to adapt as many as possible of feng shui's tenets to your own particular circumstance. But remember that it is almost impossible to get any house or apartment feng shui perfect. There will always be things causing the feng shui of the house to be less than completely auspicious. Thus every home will have its share of wrong corners, overhead beams, protruding corners, unbalanced outside elevations, inauspiciously shaped rooms and so forth. It is difficult to get main doors facing the optimum direction; many homes have their staircase directly facing the front door, and bedrooms are usually badly affected by the location of the toilet. Indeed, almost every home will have a troublesome toilet that impacts negatively on some area of life or other.

When you enter the world of feng shui, you will be confronted with a hundred different features that spell bad luck . . . and sometimes the purported cure for the inauspicious feature will be extremely hard or inconvenient to implement. You truly should not fret. Even when you read my books and note with horror that your home exactly corresponds to my example of an inauspiciously laid out home, you should not fret. I find that it is a fairly common occurrence among those new to the subject to worry or panic. They then rush out to engage the first feng shui master they read about and end up resenting the fact that the solution given is so simple or they could have got it from a good book.

Almost every negative arrangement, construction or decorative feature which may be causing problems can be corrected. Of course, some problems will always be easier to deal with than others. Just as some solutions are more obvious than others. But in feng shui practice there is room for the creative solution that is carefully thought out based on the fundamental basis upon which all feng shui guidelines are formulated.

If you feel you are suffering from bad feng shui take a methodical approach, carefully diagnosing and listing all the things that are wrong and then systematically attending to them. Many feng shui problems are not difficult to spot. So this type of defensive approach should first be undertaken before any thoughts of creating abundance by enhancing your feng shui can be considered. A single negative feng shui feature has the potential to completely destroy all carefully laid out feng shui enhancers.

Developing an inner awareness to feng shui

The first thing to do is to develop the feng shui eye. This takes a certain amount of practice. It is useful to learn what to look out for, and then go around your neighbourhood carefully studying the shapes of houses, the angles of roof lines and the way buildings and houses are built next to each other. When you start to practise like this, your subconscious mind picks up a great deal of information that it then proceeds to file away.

You must also learn the nuances of feng shui diagnosis. For example, no feature standing by itself is intrinsically bad. Thus roads, buildings and other structures are not inherently inauspicious. These structures and features only become bad feng shui for you when they are positioned in such a way that they are hurting you or your home. On the other hand, so called auspicious feng shui features can sometimes cause problems if they are positioned in a way that is inauspicious to your home.

To practise feng shui effectively for yourself, learn to see the big picture. I always advise taking the helicopter view so that you can appreciate the larger perspective. This does not always require you to ride in a helicopter to look at your house or apartment block. But it does call for a good and accurate drawing of your house layout and then meditating on it until you can see the house in the context of the surroundings.

Later, as you become more adept at the practice and start to apply such advanced feng shui formulas as flying star feng shui or eight mansions feng shui you will discover that formula techniques stay silent on the physical landscapes of your house. This can be misleading to the amateur practitioner. It does not mean you do not factor landscape feng shui into your practice. You must understand that the most well-formulated feng shui house can have its feng shui destroyed by a particularly fierce feng shui feature present in the surrounding environment. In feng shui jargon, a poison arrow will destroy even the most well feng shuied house.

On balance, therefore, you will always have to decide which feature to build upon and which school of feng shui to follow. In recent years, because of the proliferation of different feng shui methods this is something you will have to address.

I find that the best way to differentiate between authentic feng shui practitioners is to check the background of the person offering his/her feng shui services. Do some discreet research. Find out if feng shui has helped the person achieve all the things he/she is promising to create for you through feng shui. If he/she does not appear to be benefiting from good feng shui you would do well to find someone else. Feng shui always works when you get it right. It is not a spiritual practice that is dependent on some magical powers, nor is it dependent on the size of your own house.

Good feng shui locations

Classical feng shui talks about the green dragon and the white tiger, two of four celestial animals used in landscape symbolism to assist practitioners search out plots of land that promise auspicious good luck. In feng shui terms, the dragon is epitomized by elevated land-forms – ranges of hilly land that are gently undulating. The white tiger of the west exudes protective energies that enhance the presence of the green dragon. According to master practitioners, where the dragon resides there too will be the tiger. It is not therefore necessary to activate the tiger inside the home.

Dragons and tigers are found by carefully studying hill and mountain formations. The curves of elevated landforms, the green of the vegetation, the colour of the soil, and the contours of surround-ings – all offer clues to the location of the dragon's lair. Flat plains that have no gradation of slopes, or steep hills, or places where vegetation appears dead and dry usually do not house the feng shui dragon.

Dragons are not easy to locate since they rest, hidden and quietly sleeping among undulating hills, although the formation of these hills seldom offer clear indications of the presence of the celestial creature. Also, different hill shapes often exist side by side, making the search difficult. Practising feng shui masters, however, do offer vital clues that may be followed. They advise the amateur practitioner to search for cloistered corners where the vegetation is verdant, where gentle breezes blow and where the air smells good. There should also be evidence of shade and sunlight that reflect the balance of yin and yang.

Dragons do not live at the tops of hills where there is little protection against the elements. Such locations are best avoided. Dragons also cannot be found in places that appear threatened by overhanging ridges and outcrops of rocks that create malevolent and hostile vibrations. Again, this sort of landscape is best avoided.

And where the air is musty and damp, where the soil is rocky and hard, there also can be no healthy life-giving breath. Once again, places like these do not represent good feng shui. They are places where the dragon cannot reside.

Feng shui masters advise that you should look instead for land where there is evidence of lush green grass or vegetation. Where the soil is fertile and the air is pleasant and sweet smelling. These offer clues to the existence of the vital life-giving breath. On such hillsides the elusive feng shui green dragon could well be hidden, coiled in close embrace with the white tiger.

Usually the dragon hills lie to the east (or the left side of the site) and the tiger hills the west, or right side. The dragon hills are also slightly higher than the tiger hills. According to the descriptions given in the old manuals, the place of greatest accumulation of cosmic breath is where the green dragon is said to be copulating with the white tiger. Where these two creatures meet in a coiled embrace is the spot to build your house because this is where the dragon exudes the greatest amount of its cosmic breath, what the Chinese refer to as sheng chi, the breath that brings harmony, prosperity, health and long life.

In practical terms, the most auspicious configuration is when these two ranges curve round like an armchair or horseshoe. When you see such a hill formation, and the vegetation in the area is also lush and healthy, it is a sure indication that you are on the right track. Such places are very auspicious sites. If there is also a clean and slow moving river in front, the feng shui luck indicated is even more magnificent. To make one's home on such a site promises a life rich in material, physical and spiritual benefits. Abundant good luck and wealth are promised for many generations.

This sort of hill configuration, which resembles an armchair formation or a horseshoe, also features the presence of black turtle hills behind the house, and a small hillock in front, which represents the crimson phoenix – symbolizing a footstool for the inhabitants to rest their tired feet. These four animals – the dragon, tiger, turtle and phoenix – are collectively regarded as the four celestial animals of the Chinese Zodiac.

In real life such naturally excellent feng shui sites are hard to locate, or acquire. In the old days when wealthy mandarins built their family mansions on large tracts of land against hillsides, the green dragon/white tiger symbolism was held to be vitally important. But it is a guideline that is especially difficult to follow in the context of the modern day environment, when people live more in towns and cities than on hillsides.

It was partly this practical difficulty that prompted modern feng shui masters to adapt the principles of landscape feng shui to present-day practice. Thus in Hong Kong, buildings are deemed to represent dragons and tigers, while roads are viewed in the same way as olden

Land formation

Feng shui masters advise that land on the east side of your house should always be higher than the land on the west side; and that it is preferable to have some slightly higher land behind your house thereby giving your back support.

There should also be some amount of flat empty space in front of the house, to allow the good chi to settle and accumulate. These guidelines simulate the armchair formation thereby allowing inhabitants of the household to live harmoniously with the environment, and benefiting from the chi that then accumulates in front of the house. Where the back support is missing, planting a clump of solid trees that serve the same purpose can further simulate it. And for those eager to tap into the wealth-bringing chi of rivers and waterways, it is also possible to create an artificial waterway in front of the house.

days' waterways. Interpretations of the ancient feng shui classics have taken on modern day perspectives.

The auspicious green dragon/white tiger formation can also be artificially created, and be just as effective in creating favourable chi flows. It is in this context that feng shui becomes so exciting.

Poison arrows and the killing breath

Feng shui also warns against shar chi or the killing breath. This brings misfortune and a great deal of bad luck, and is caused by the presence of secret poison arrows. Poison arrows are created by pointed, angled and sharp objects that seem to be aimed directly at a house, and especially at its main door. Examples of poison arrows are straight roads, rivers or railways lines that seem to be aimed directly at the main front door. Or they could be caused by the triangular shaped roof lines caused by neighbours' homes, or by the sharp edge of big buildings. These are very strong poison arrows that can cause severe bad luck that manifest in the form of ill health, sickness, and even death.

Examples of other arrows that can affect households is when a single tree trunk, a telephone pole, or a transmission tower is located directly in front of the main door. The pernicious effect of all these poison arrows must be deflected, dissolved or diffused. Feng shui recommends several ways of doing this, and they have to do with blocking or redirecting the shar chi away from the house. Thus main door directions can be shifted, trees planted, or walls built to combat poison arrows.

Even if you do not know very much about feng shui, just by being aware of the dangers of poison arrows and consciously avoiding their ill effects should help you avoid some of the dangers caused by bad feng shui.

Learning to identify poison arrows is a useful first step in the practice of feng shui. There are many different ways of developing this expertise but the best method is to train yourself to be very observant. Take note of your surroundings. Develop awareness to the different buildings and roads that you see each day as you go to work. Look at the angles and sharp lines that are caused by the edges of buildings and then use your eye to note where and how they are hitting at the entrances of other buildings, shops or houses. Feel the overpowering energy of very tall or heavy buildings.

Check out the neighbourhood where you live and tune in to the different types of energy given off by the different houses you see. After some time you will begin to notice that some houses look more prosperous and happier than others. Try to identify the good and bad feng shui features of every house. If you train yourself to look out for poison arrows and become really good at identifying the structures that are sending out negative and killing energies you will have learnt and mastered a vital part of feng shui practice.

You should be very exact and precise in your mental analysis. Do not allow your mind to go off in all directions. It is not necessary to be paranoid about angular, sharp or triangular structures even though these are usually the most harmful. Instead, take a relaxed attitude towards identifying poison arrows and once you have identified them see if they are hurting your home. If they are, use your imagination and creativity for the best way to diffuse the straight energy being sent to your main door. There is always a solution to the problem of poison arrows.

If there is a particularly difficult feng shui problem confronting your house and you want to find a way to overcome it, the best way is to think of how to block the offending structure from view. It is for this reason that feng shui practitioners are so fond of using mirrors. Reflecting the structure back with a mirror is usually such a convenient way but you may not want to reflect the bad flow of energy back to the house opposite. In such a situation, coming up with an alternative cure is perfectly acceptable. For example, if a straight road is pointing directly at your main door, either change the location of your door or plant some trees to block out the road or build a wall.

Developing a reverence for the earth

Perhaps the best approach to using feng shui is to develop a genuine reverence for the energies of the earth, and for mother earth herself. Feng shui is the luck of the earth, and when we use feng shui we are really tapping into its auspicious energies. Mankind can manipulate these energies, so that they flow auspiciously and bring abundance rather than ill fortune. But we can do this only if we understand the importance of harmony and balance.

Harmony of earth energy has to do with the earth's interactions with the other elements that make up the Universe. Earth is one of five elements. The other elements that continually interact with earth and with each other are water, fire, metal and wood. According to feng shui, every object, circumstance, direction, season and so forth represents one of the five elements – fire, earth, metal, water and wood. Each element on its own is neither good nor bad. Every element

Water, fire, metal and wood: how they interact with earth

Water has the potential to overflow and overwhelm the earth, just as the earth can also overcome water. Indeed, if anything can destroy water it is earth. Yet water can also enrich the earth so that together, earth and water create the circumstances for trees and plants to grow. Water and earth together therefore can create the abundance of growth and would be very hospitable to the element of wood.

The element of fire is said to be the one element that can create and produce earth. Fire does not exist on its own, nor can it be stored. It has to be produced. But fire provides warmth to the earth and during winter months fire becomes a welcome complement to the earth.

Within the earth there is the element of metal. Thus earth is said to be the producer of metal. This is the hidden abundance of earth – it has the potential to create gold which, of course,

symbolizes wealth and great abundance. Indeed, the Chinese word for metal is kum or gold. The two are considered to be the same. But metal is cold and unbending. There is no life in metal. It is the only element that has no movement and no life, unlike the other elements.

The only element which has a life of its own is wood. This element is the symbol of plant life. It depends on the earth for sustenance and for a home. Plants and trees grow in the earth using up the goodness that the earth offers. The wood element is the only one that benefits from all the other four elements, using up the nourishment provided by the earth, water and metal elements to grow, and then depending on the fire element to cause itself to break out into blooms. It is the fire of the sun that causes plants to produce food and flowers which can be harvested.

also has a positive countenance and a negative condition, just as every element has a yin countenance or a yang appearance.

Each of these elements has a special relationship with earth and with each other and understanding the cycle of the five elements is central to the practice of feng shui. In the conventional theory of the five elements, there is a productive cycle as well as a destructive cycle. These cycles offer a simple yet effective first level analysis of whether the energies that surround any space are in harmony or not. Further discussion of the ways to use the five elements to create harmony for the home appears on pages 46–8 and 140–44.

The productive cycle

In the productive cycle, water produces wood which produces fire which produces earth which produces metal which produces water. Thus elements are said to be compatible, and therefore harmonious when one produces the other. Using this logic therefore, when your room is decorated in colours that suggest the wood element (green or brown) then a complementary colour, which will enhance the wood, would be blue or black because these are the colours of water. This simple example demonstrates that it is not any element *per se* which brings good or bad luck. It is the way the various elements represented in any space interact with each other that creates the good or bad luck.

Under certain circumstances, the presence of all five elements is said to be excellent feng shui because this suggests the abundance of the whole. Thus in parts of the house that correspond to compass directions that belong to the earth or wood elements, the presence of all five elements is said to be auspicious.

The parts of the home that correspond to the earth element are the southwest corner, the northeast corner and the centre. When all five elements are present in these parts of the home, earth energies are said to be at their most potent.

The parts of the house that correspond to the wood element are the east and southeast. The wood element represents growth, and when all five elements are present, wood grows at its most efficient and fastest.

Here is where abundance is created. It is therefore an auspicious arrangement to ensure the presence of all five elements in the east and southeast.

The destructive cycle

In the destructive cycle of the elements, fire destroys metal which destroys wood which destroys earth which destroys water which destroys fire.

Elements are said to be incompatible when one destroys the other. Thus if you decorate your living room in red and blue the elements are clashing because water destroys fire. The effect becomes worse when there is a great deal of blue in a room which corresponds to the south corner of the house since the south belongs to the element of fire. A blue colour scheme in the south is said to put out the auspicious energy of fire.

Another example is the placement of red in rooms that belong to the metal element. Such rooms are those located in the west or north-west of the home. Red symbolizes fire which destroys metal. Placing a red colour scheme in the metal corners of your home will kill off the luck in those rooms.

A great deal of feng shui has to do with element analysis and it is essential to understand how the elements interact with each other. Indeed, in the Far East, feng shui masters who understand the many nuances of the way elements interact with each other are those who eventually make a name for themselves as being excellent feng shui masters. This is because in addition to using the cycles to analyse the feng shui of the elements, it is equally important to go deeper.

Thus while fire is said to destroy metal, we can also say that it is only with fire that metal can be transformed into real objects of value. Without fire, metal could not possibly be made into valuable ornaments. Likewise, water is said to cause wood to grow yet when there is too much water, the wood rots and dies.

And again, when you think a little deeper about the relationship between metal and wood – two incompatible elements – you will see that while metal is said to destroy wood, we can see that big metal destroys big wood yet small metal enhances big wood. How? Wood gets fashioned into furniture with small metal implements and tools.

In another example of incompatible elements, this time water and fire, we see that while water puts out the fire, there can also be a situation when the fire turns water into steam which represents power. Steam is a powerful force indeed and this can be harnessed to cause great abundance!

Applying five element analysis to the practical applications of feng shui therefore requires greater depth of thinking than is at first obvious. For the amateur practitioner, however, understanding the cycles of the elements and learning about the element associations and representations should offer further food for thought.

Understanding chi – the cosmic breath

Central to the understanding of feng shui is the concept of the cosmic breath of the celestial dragon. When the energies of any space are in harmony, the cosmic breath of that space are said to be auspicious. This breath is referred to as the chi of the environment. This chi can be beneficial or harmful. Thus beneficial breath was termed as sheng chi while killing breath was called shar chi.

Chi itself is said to be the life force, or energy, that pervades man's existence. Chi is created when a monk sits in meditation and breathes correctly; or when a kung fu expert gives a well-aimed blow. Or when a master calligrapher makes a singularly artistic brushstroke. Chi is also created in nature by the gentle meandering flow of water; by the shape of a mountain, or by the symmetry of landforms in the environment.

Thus, places that enjoyed good feng shui were often described as localities where the beneficial cosmic breath – the sheng chi – was present in the greatest abundance. This invisible presence of the cosmic breath would, in turn, bring material abundance to anyone dwelling in the vicinity of the breath. In the old days when the language of feng shui was couched in a great deal of symbolic metaphors, reference was made to the celestial animals – particularly to the green dragon of the east and the white tiger of the west – to describe such places of good feng shui. Dragons and tigers thus referred to hill and mountain ranges that undulated in the landscapes. In addition, the presence of vegetation and water also offered clues to the amount of beneficial chi hovering around.

The cosmic chi of the green dragon is its breath and it is where this valuable breath can be created and accumulated that great good fortune can be tapped. This cosmic chi is the source of peace and prosperity, abundant wealth, honour and great good fortune. In areas where this chi exists and accumulates, homes and abodes will benefit the household through several generations. Businesses located in places with good chi flows will expand and grow.

Chi must never be allowed to be scattered or blown away. If this happens there can be no good luck. In places where fast, strong winds blow, chi is scattered and dispersed. Usually 'chi rides the wind and disperses'. Excessively windy sites are thus unfavourable. When bounded by water, however, chi halts and accumulates. Thus places with the presence of water are usually auspicious locations.

Naturally, the quality of the water also affects the quality of the chi created. Fast flowing waters like straight rivers carry chi away as soon as it is created. And polluted rivers can hardly be expected to create the beneficial breath. At the same time, chi must not be allowed to stagnate or grow stale or tired. This, too, will cause all good luck to dissipate.

Good feng shui therefore is dependent on how much chi is present, as well as whether there continues to be a source of it. In places where it accumulates on a regular basis, feng shui luck will be auspicious. In places where it stagnates, grows stale or is rapidly dispersed, feng shui luck cannot be good. The ideal situation is to ensure your home has access to or is near a good strong supply and flow of chi. If the natural landscape does not have such a supply, you can build an artificial simulation of the kind of environment that generates strong amounts of chi. Artificial ponds and hills work just as well as the natural thing and when they are properly landscaped according to good feng shui guidelines they too will bring great good fortune.

The essence of good feng shui is to trap the cosmic breath flowing through any site, and create a landscape that encourages it to accumulate without it becoming stagnant. Where the dragon's breath can be contained or where a permanent supply can be built up there will definitely be wealth, prosperity and abundance. Feng shui offers the guidelines and methods for harnessing the dragon's breath. The accepted theory is that this will not be where there are straight vertical ridges. Waterways and roads should be slow and meandering rather than straight and the site must be protected from harsh winds.

2 Creating abundance with feng shui

'Successful feng shui requires a
Multi-dimensional approach,
There are many variations
To the lay of the land, the orientations
Of rivers and mountains and valleys
Stay in tune with the environment
And let the winds and waters guide you . . .'

TO BE SUCCESSFUL at using feng shui, you should not limit your-self to a one-dimensional approach. Feng shui is a collection of rich and profound techniques that offer a wide variety of options for the practitioner. This is a science that has evolved over three thousand years, and in its journey through the Imperial dynasties of China, down the centuries and into the modern metropolis age of today, the master practitioners have refined, expanded and adapted the guidelines of feng shui to suit the changing situations of the times.

In this last century, a great deal of feng shui secret formulas left China and travelled with Chinese immigrants to places like Hong Kong and Taiwan. In these foreign lands, feng shui masters developed new guidelines to deal with city environments and experimented with various interpretations of ancient formulas. They discovered different ways of achieving the same end and because of the infinite variety of spatial situations, sometimes what worked in one territory worked less well, or better, in another.

Feng shui as practised by the Chinese in Taiwan, for instance, differs to some extent from the feng shui practised by the Chinese of Hong Kong. These differences reflect variances in dialect interpretations of ancient texts. But they may also have been due to the particular spe-cializations of masters who fled to these two places, bringing with them their own formulas.

At the same time, there are any number of variations to the shape, layout and orientations of homes everywhere. The average person will find it impossible to implement all the feng shui recommendations given in a single book, or under a single method of feng shui. It is also not always possible to deal adequately with feng shui problems, because of the way homes have been built. Modern city type homes bear no resemblance to the homes of olden days when feng shui guidelines were first formulated.

Master practitioners from China who emigrated to Taiwan and Hong Kong have devised modern day interpretations to old formulas and depending on whom you learn your feng shui from, you will find yourself using one formula more than another. There are thus different ways of dealing with feng shui problems and you should try to have a working knowledge of these alternative methods. In the same way, there are also different methods for energizing the space to create wealth and abundance.

Who you choose to learn your feng shui from should be a clever decision. An excellent way to judge is to look at the circumstances of the person offering his or her version of feng shui. I have never believed in learning feng shui from masters who themselves live in situations of material and spiritual poverty. How can they help you when they cannot even help themselves?

When I was researching feng shui techniques I sought out master practitioners who had obviously benefited from their craft. I was also very particular about knowing the reasons behind recommendations given since the basis of doing anything to my space had to also appeal to my own common sense. I urge you to take the same approach. It is only when you are convinced that you can undertake feng shui changes with conviction and have a positive anticipation to the results.

The practice of feng shui requires creativity and ingenuity. By understanding the rationale that lies behind feng shui recommendations, you will be able to generate various alternative solutions that best suit your particular circumstance. It is this, more than anything, which originally made me embark on doing my own feng shui. I knew that my life and my success meant more to me than to any feng shui master. I was more careful and circumspect in my practice. You should be like that too.

I discovered that having access to the use of formula feng shui broadened my options considerably. Knowing different formulas and techniques allows a more thorough and comprehensive approach. The formulas can then be combined with the practice of landscape or form school feng shui.

Feng shui formulas

Formula feng shui adds a vital dimension to the concept of the beneficial breath. For instance, the eight mansions school (the Pa Kua Lo Shu formula that is based on individual dates of birth) offers additional methods for individuals who, having found a site of good feng shui, can then fine tune the way they orientate their abodes and dwelling places. Applying compass formulas that are deemed auspicious according to the formula allows you to arrange the personalized chi of your presence to complement the beneficial chi of the environment. This takes the practice of feng shui a step deeper into the study and alignments of the cosmic breath to synchronize personal energies with that of the environment.

The eight mansions school is a particularly potent feng shui formula because it offers precise ways of implementing specific feng shui orientations, making the practice easy because it leaves subjectivity out of the process.

Eight mansions feng shui spells out the most auspicious way of orientating the main door for a particular individual. In addition, it offers detailed directions for the orientation of the sleeping head and the positioning of the sitting direction. The result is that the cosmic breath of the space is being tapped in a way that is aligned in the most beneficial way for the person.

A second formula, which can be applied to feng shui practice, is that of the flying stars formula. This is an excellent tool for revealing the significance of the time dimension on the cosmic breath of any space. The flying stars formula enables practitioners to calculate the natal chart of houses based on when they were built or significantly renovated. These natal charts allow for the time factor to be incorporated into the spatial analysis of the feng shui of any home. It thus results in a more thorough application of feng shui tools.

Not having it, however, does not negate recommendations that are based on other methods and formulas of feng shui. The effect of the time dimension must always be taken account of since it offers explanations for bad luck befalling a house with good feng shui. This is during a particular time which may be a week, a month or a year depending on which stars are inauspicious.

Despite these introductory remarks about formula feng shui, note that homes that are built and designed according to spatial feng shui guidelines will always enjoy the beneficial cosmic breath. Any bad luck or misfortune brought on by the flying stars is usually a temporary phenomenon. It is therefore sufficient to know which compass locations signify extreme misfortune during each year

The forces of wind and water

The existence of different schools of feng shui can cause confusion, especially when it is compounded by the different interpretations on practical applications being propounded by those who have insufficient experience in the practice of feng shui. Recommendations often seem to be contradictory, and especially so when the approach taken is overly simplistic. I have found, however, that when you do not lose sight of the fundamentals, it is not difficult to incorporate all the different authentic schools into the way you use feng shui to design your space.

Remember that feng shui is predicated on the intrinsic power of the winds and the waters on the physical environment. The quality and characteristics of these two forces are affected by the way the five elements interact, by the compass directions of their flow and most of all by the intrinsic energies that lie at the heart of wind and water.

The forces of wind and water have a yin as well as a yang aspect, and as a result everything caused by these two forces also has a yin and yang aspect. The way yin and yang interacts therefore has a bearing on whether the energies that pervade a space are beneficial or not.

The yin yang symbol

Yang is white and bright, daylight, warmth and activity, sunshine, summer and life itself. The dot of yin energy is what gives existence to yang.

Yin is black, darkness, the night, winter, cold, death and silence. Yin aspects must always be present but they should never dominate in houses of the living. Too much yin energy will cause negative feng shui.

Thus when you use feng shui principles and formulas, always apply the test of the five elements and that of the yin yang cosmology. The five-element analysis will ensure there is harmony in your environment while the yin yang examination ensures there is a balance of the forces that express the way of the Universe. Together they address the twin requirements of harmony and balance into the living space.

(see the table left) and to observe the recommended safeguards for that year. For example, during the lunar year 1998, a bad flying star afflicted the cosmic breath of the northeast corner of any home. To counteract this I recommended that a five-rod wind chime be placed in the northeast corner through the course of the year. Afflicted corners change from year to year, and which corner this is depends on the way the stars fly around the Lo Shu square. In the year 1999, the afflicted corner is the south and so it is a good idea to place an urn filled with water in the south corner of your house. Change the water regularly. More information about the flying stars is given on pages 104–5 with specific relevance to health.

Defining the parameters of your space

Before applying all the methods for creating abundance contained in this book you will need to define the parameters of your space. This is the preparation part of practising feng shui and it is important to do this properly and correctly since all of your analysis will be based on the directions you take and the way your space has been demarcated. This is the technical side of the whole exercise and you require two tools to do it: a Western compass and the Lo Shu square.

The compass

Invest in a good Western compass, preferably one with the directions marked out in degrees. You will find that to get feng shui recommendations to work it is necessary to be accurate in taking the compass direction readings. While many feng shui masters still use the Chinese Luo Pan to take their readings, this is not necessary for the amateur practitioner. I do all my feng shui work with a Western compass simply because I find these compasses easier to read and much better constructed. They are also more accurate. If you live in a part of the world where the ground has seismic activity you may have to get a stronger surveyor's compass.

Taking a compass reading can be tricky. I recommend you take three readings and use the average as the one you use for your feng shui demarcations. If the readings vary by more than 15 degrees, it can mean the energies in the room are a little out of balance. This can usually be corrected by looking at where you have placed all your electronic equipment such as your TV and Hi-Fi equipment.

If, after re-arranging the equipment, you still get variations in your readings that exceed 15 degrees it suggests that you may be affected by underground ley lines. Move a metre (yard) to the right or left and try again. The three readings should be taken as follows:

- just inside the front door
- a metre (yard) inside the house, measured from the front door
- 4.5m (5yd) inside the house, also measured from the front door.

At all times, take the reading from the inside of the door looking out and in this book all references to directions are assumed to be measured in the same way. Once you know the exact direction your door faces you will be able to apply all the compass formulas of feng shui. Also, once you know what direction the main door faces you will be in a position to mark out the eight compass directions of your house.

Generally speaking, the direction that your main door faces is regarded as the front of your house, and ideally the front of your house should be facing the nearest main road that lies in the vicinity of your home. Usually when houses (and business premises) directly face the main road it is said to bring good feng shui luck because of the large amounts of yang energy that is being generated by the busy activity of a main road. The downside, of course, is that when you live too near to main roads it is very noisy.

Superimposing the Lo Shu square

After determining the door direction, the next thing to establish is the door location. This requires you to divide the layout plan of your house into a grid of nine equal squares (or rectangles) by superimposing the Lo Shu square onto a plan of the house.

Superimposing the Lo Shu grid would be a very simple thing to do if all houses were a perfect square. Unfortunately, this is seldom the

The Lo Shu square or grid

Many Chinese of Taoist origin believe this to be the magic square. In feng shui, the sequence of numbers provides the basis of many compass formulas. The use of the Lo Shu square is widely used in advanced feng shui work. For the amateur practitioner it is sufficient to memorize the sequence of the numbers around the grid and which compass directions the numbers correspond to.

4	9	2
3	5	7
8	1	6

The Lo Shu square or grid

case. Most homes have irregular shapes and missing corners. They are seldom perfect squares and rectangles.

It is also difficult to decide whether to include the garage, the gazebo and other structures in the garden. The rule of thumb is that if the rooms are not connected to the house then they are not considered to be part of it. If there is a corridor connecting the two structures and it is covered with a roof, then one big grid must be drawn to take account of the out-house as well as the corridor.

When superimposing the Lo Shu grid onto a layout plan, imagine you are looking down at the house from a helicopter. Anything that has a roof covering it is regarded as being part of the house and must thus be taken account of in the grid. Usually there will be missing corners created by the non-regular shape of houses and analysing these missing corners will help you to analyse the quality of the house feng shui.

When doing this part of the preparatory work, it is also a good idea to look at the shape of your house. Note whether you have lots of corners and whether there are any protruding corners. Examine which part of the house/apartment is most lived in, ie where family members congregate most regularly. This is usually the kitchen, family and TV rooms. These areas should always be the most auspicious corners of the home and chapters 3 and 8 expand on how you can enhance these areas.

Superimposing the Pa Kua for analysis

You now have a starting point for creating abundance with feng shui. Make several copies of the layout plan with all the directions marked and the grid drawn in and as you work through this book keep the plan nearby. You can then make notes on the recommendations that apply to your home or those areas that you wish to energize.

An easy way to identify the corners for energizing good fortune is to then superimpose the Pa Kua onto your layout plan. The Pa Kua is an eight-sided symbol of feng shui and on each side is one of eight trigrams. How these trigrams are placed around the Pa Kua determines what kind of Pa Kua it is. There are two arrangements and therefore two kinds of Pa Kuas – the yin Pa Kua and the yang Pa Kua.

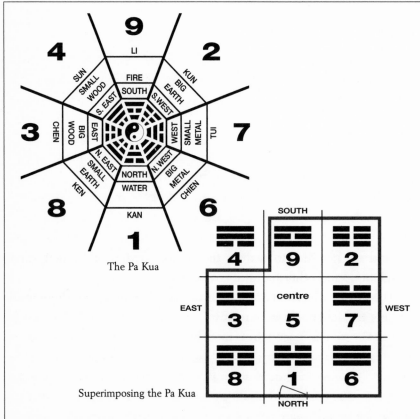

The Pa Kua

Superimposing the Pa Kua

The Pa Kua

The symbols and numbers shown around this Pa Kua are based on the Later Heaven Arrangement of the trigrams. The arrangement is the cornerstone of feng shui practice for homes and offices. You can use these representations to analyse what is required to enhance the energy of each corresponding direction.

Superimposing the Pa Kua

Superimpose the Pa Kua onto a layout plan of your home. You can do this over the whole house or for each room separately. Then you can energize the rooms using the house as the whole or energize corners of each room. The significance of the numbers should also be incorporated into your feng shui practice, eg one tortoise in the north and nine lamps in the south!

The yin Pa Kua

This form of the Pa Kua is usually hung above main doors to ward off killing energy which may be hurting the door. Such Pa Kuas are usually drawn with a red background to create strong yang energy and have a mirror in the centre. When this mirror is concave it reflects the poison arrow which it is warding off, and is thus a more hostile tool than when the mirror is convex. When this latter is the case, it absorbs the killing energy and so is not as hostile. If the mirror is flat, it is neither hostile nor friendly.

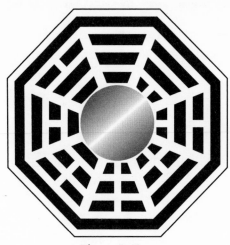

The yin Pa Kua

The yin Pa Kua

Here the trigrams are arranged in what the Chinese describe as a cyclical pattern. In this arrangement, the trigrams are placed in pairs of opposites generally referred to as the Early Heaven Arrangement. The most important trigram – *chien*, which represents heaven and the patriarch – is placed in the south and directly opposite in the north is the trigram that represents the matriarch, the trigram *kun*. These two are the ultimate yang and yin trigrams. There is thus nothing more yang than *chien* and there is nothing more yin than *kun*.

The arrangement of the trigrams in the yin Pa Kua is said to possess intrinsic heavenly power which can deflect and overcome shar chi or killing breath. Thus this trigram arrangement is the one that is placed around the Pa Kua to deflect the poison arrows of straight roads, T-junctions and other harmful structures.

The yin Pa Kua should never be displayed or hung anywhere inside the home. Nor should it be used to counter poison arrows that may be present inside the home. In destroying the shar chi of the poison arrow, it will also harm residents who inadvertently get hit by the Pa Kua. I stress this very strenuously since I know that there are people masquerading as feng shui masters who are recommending that Pa Kua mirrors be hung inside the home. Please don't do it as it is very dangerous.

The yang Pa Kua

This is the Pa Kua used for feng shui analysis. The yin Pa Kua is more suitable for yin dwellings which are the dwellings of the dead – the tombs of our ancestors. When feng shui is being done for ancestral burial sites it is the yin Pa Kua that is consulted. Yang dwellings, on the other hand, are houses of the living, and so the yang Pa Kua is used. Based on the placement of the trigrams around the yang Pa Kua, feng shui practitioners can use the symbols, elements, and other representations related to the respective trigrams and assign these meanings to each of the eight directions. It is these representations and meanings that are placed around the feng shui geomancer's compass or Luo Pan.

On the yang Pa Kua, the arrangement of the trigrams is described as being of the Later Heaven Arrangement. The trigrams reflect the premise that the relationship between the opposites of the Early Heaven Arrangement has given way to changes. Now the trigram that is placed in the south is no longer *chien* but is instead the trigram *li*, and the trigram in the north is no longer *kun* but *kan*. The ultimate yang and yin trigrams are now placed in the northwest and southwest respectively.

The yang Pa Kua

The yang Pa Kua

This form of the Pa Kua is used in the analysis of feng shui requirements for dwellings of the living (as opposed to the houses of the dead). The arrangement of the trigrams is different: the trigram placed in the south is the trigram li, *which symbolizes fire, and the trigram placed north is* kan, *which signifies water.*

The illustration of the yang Pa Kua shown opposite offers several layers of representations, which will help the amateur practitioner. For instance, if you look at the compass direction south, you will see that the corresponding trigram is *li*. The element of this trigram is fire. Thus the element associated with the south will be fire and if you want to make the south corner of your room more auspicious, one way of doing it is to place a bright red lamp in that corner. This enhances the fire element of the corner thereby strengthening it. Incidentally, for those of you living in the southern hemisphere you will see that the reason the south is associated with the element fire has nothing to do with the winds or the location of the equator as has been speculated by some feng shui writers. It is the placement of the trigram *li* in the south which creates the link between the fire element and the south.

Likewise, the north is associated with cold and with the element of water because the trigram that is placed in the north under the arrangement is *kan*, whose element is water. Hence to enhance the north corner of any house or any room, you can use water. Placing a water feature will achieve this end.

Understanding the symbols of the Pa Kua

The Pa Kua has a whole range of symbolic meanings assigned to each of the eight directions. Cleverly analysing these meanings is the first step to enhancing your living space to generate good feelings. If you do nothing else save use the Pa Kua's symbols to give you the clues for energizing the eight corners of your home, you will succeed in creating a perfectly harmonious home that generates a feeling of relaxed well-being. There will be many different opportunities for you to enhance your life and you will enjoy good health and happy relationships. You will also enjoy greater material wealth and benefit from better incomes.

The Pa Kua is itself a very powerful symbol but around its eight sides, which signify the four primary and four secondary directions, are additional symbols that can be incorporated into the feng shui planning of any home. The idea is to systematically attend to every room in the house. Use these symbols also to enhance the energies and cosmic breath of each corner.

The south (the trigram li)

The element of the south is fire and so this is the place of warmth and heat. The south becomes lucky during the season of summer. This is a very yang direction and the colours associated with the south are usually red, or very bright yellow. Everything to do with fire is associated with this direction including the lightning in the sky. This is the place of the middle daughter whose bedroom if placed here will bring good fortune to her. The south is a direction that benefits the females more than the males, more suitable for daughters than sons. The celestial animal of the south is the crimson phoenix that brings wonderful opportunities for advancement and rise in status. Simply displaying the phoenix in the south brings enormous good fortune.

The north (the trigram kan)

The element of the north is water and so this is the place of cold and stillness. The season is winter. The dominant colour of the north is black which is very yin. Blues and deep purples are very auspicious for the north. Everything to do with the cold and with water, including lakes, rivers, and waterways, is associated with this direction which is the place of the middle son. The north of the house is better for sons than for daughters. The symbol of the celestial animal is the tortoise, and the simple act of placing a tortoise in the north brings great good fortune for the whole family.

The east (the trigram chen)

Here the element is wood and this is the best place in the house for the eldest son. In fact, all the sons of the family will do well when placed in the east. If you have only one child and she is a daughter she will also flourish in this east room. This is because the element here is wood and the east signifies growth. The east is also the place of the auspicious green dragon. To enhance these corners of the house use plenty of lush verdant plants.

The west (the trigram tui)

This is a place of joy. Here is where gold is found and the element of the west is metal. The dominant colour is white. This is the place best suited for the young women of the family. If the youngest daughter is placed here she will reap beneficial energies. The west is also the place of the white tiger in feng shui lore.

But it is not advisable to display a tiger here since we do not want to energize the tiger. Having a tiger symbol in the house is not universally auspicious since only people born either in the years of the tiger or dragon can sustain the powerful energies of this fierce creature.

The southeast (the trigram sun)

The element of this corner is small wood. This is a corner which symbolizes the wind of feng shui. It is the corner of wealth for the wind is believed to bring prosperity via the southeast direction. To energize this corner of the house it is best to use plants and flowers. Lights are also excellent as lights signify a successful harvest. The southeast is the place of the eldest daughter.

The southwest (the trigram kun)

This is the place of the matriarch and the element is that of big earth. The southwest is thus the place of the big earth mama. This is a very important part of the house since the place of the matriarch in feng shui connotes the focal point of all human relationships and happiness. If the southwest of your house is afflicted either because it is missing, or if a toilet is placed there, or if it houses the storeroom – all the residents in the whole house will suffer. Marriages will become unhappy. Siblings will not get along and all love relationships will be seriously affected in a negative way. This is because the mother is regarded as central to the family unit. Always look after the southwest of your home if you want to maintain happy relationships within the family and with lovers.

The northeast (the trigram ken*)*

This is the place of stillness, the mountain. The element is earth. This is the place which is best suited for the youngest son of the family. The northeast is the best location to place a wealth vase since this suggests the symbolism of gold inside the mountain. Placing a wealth vase in a cupboard in this corner guarantees that the luck of the family will get better with the passing of time. It also guarantees that the family house will always stay with the family. It will not be lost.

The northwest (the trigram chien*)*

This is the place of the father, the patriarch, the breadwinner. Like the southwest the northwest is a vital and most important corner of the house. If it is adversely affected by having a toilet placed there the family fortunes will suffer as a result of the patriarch suffering losses. You should always ensure that this part of the house is well taken care of. It is not necessary to keep this corner too well lit. This is because the northeast is represented by the element of big metal and the fire element destroys metal. The best colours for this corner are thus metallic or white.

Combining earth luck with mankind luck

Before going further, one question you might want to have answered is how long it takes for feng shui changes or enhancers to work. There is no straight answer to this question. I have seen feng shui take up to 18 months before bringing real and specific opportunities to a couple whose feng shui I did sometime ago. But most of the time when feng shui is done properly I have watched it work its special brand of magic almost immediately. Usually if you do things correctly and you do not inadvertently overlook something, feng shui brings positive results very quickly.

But feng shui must be seen in proper perspective. Feng shui is only one third in the trinity of luck. Three types of luck – heaven luck, earth luck and mankind luck – rule the fortunes of man. Heaven luck is out of our control. This is one's destiny and fate. It can be likened to one's karma. Heaven luck exerts a very powerful and pervasive effect on one's destiny. It is great if you have excellent heaven luck. This means you are born into a reasonably fortunate situation with all your senses intact and living in a part of the world not afflicted by war, poverty and extremes of weather. Just being born human and having the opportunity to get educated means that most of us have reasonably good heaven luck.

Although we have no control over our heaven luck, we can endeavour to improve our circumstances and create a life of abundance for ourselves if we focus on the luck that we can control. We can control the luck from the earth through practising feng shui and we can control mankind luck by controlling the power of our own attitudes and mind. In fact, if we set out to systematically take good care of these two types of luck, the sky truly would be the limit.

By creating good feng shui in your living space, you will be setting the scenario for wonderful opportunities to come into your life. Exciting new ventures will find their way to your doorstep. In relationships you will find yourself meeting new people. At work you will experience new situations unfolding in your favour. All of these developments, however, become like nothing if you do not then exert effort to transform them into the kind of abundance you want.

Earth luck must go hand in hand with mankind luck. Only then can you enhance your overall life. Even if you were born into situations that place you at a disadvantage you can use feng shui and your mind to help you leap-frog into a life of true abundance.

Purifying the living space

The last part of the preparation for creating abundance is to familiarize yourself with a safe method of purifying your living space. Not all houses require purification, but every house will benefit from having the energies inside the home swept clean from lingering stagnant energy.

I usually do space purification once a week and I do this simply by opening all the windows of my home and turning on all the fans. This causes the energy inside the house to be refreshed by outside air flowing in. Having all the windows open allows the air to flow right through the rooms. Leave the windows open for about an hour. It is best to choose a day when the sun is shining brightly since this will be a strong yang day. Fresh yang energy is invigorated by the bright sunshine and so the energies that flow into the home will be precious. It is also excellent to purify the home with clean energy after a rainfall as this brings in air that has been cleansed and energized by the rain.

A symbolic cleaning of all surfaces should follow space purification. Use a white cloth that has been soaked in water left out in the sun. Wipe the surfaces of your doors, windows and furniture. Also symbolically wipe the floors. Cleansing of the air inside your home will attract the good sheng chi and it is worth doing this on a regular basis. Then once every quarter you might also want to do a full-scale purification of the energies.

This time, in addition to opening the windows, open all the doors of your store rooms and cupboards. Let the stale air out and the good clean fresh air in. Then perform one of the following two rituals around the whole house carefully moving from room to room.

1 Purifying with incense. Use an incense holder and burn some scented incense which also sends up smoke and move from one door to another starting with the main door and ending with the back door. Move the incense holder all round the opening of the door. Do the same for the windows. When you have finished with the doors and the windows, place some more incense in the holder and move around the rooms, making sure you purify the corners and dark spaces of the home. Use special incense made from herbs and plants that come from high in the mountains or other places where the energies are pure and powerful.

2 The other space purification ritual makes use of tinkling sounds to cleanse the energies of the home. You can use a bell or better yet a wind chime with a pure sound. I prefer a singing bowl because the

sound that comes from it is very pure and fine. This creates such wonderful, fresh, growth energy that I do this singing bowl purification once every month.

When you undertake space purification regularly like this you will feel your spirits being uplifted. The energies around the house become light and less heavy and there is a feeling of relaxed happiness. Everyone is less quarrelsome and much happier. I recommend it very highly.

3 An abundance of personal growth

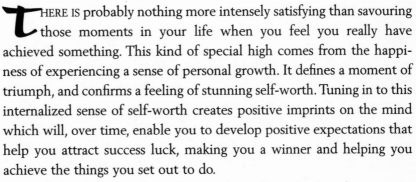

'Let feng shui be
Your life-long friend;
So that
Seeing with feng shui eyes
Become second nature . . .'

THERE IS probably nothing more intensely satisfying than savouring those moments in your life when you feel you really have achieved something. This kind of special high comes from the happiness of experiencing a sense of personal growth. It defines a moment of triumph, and confirms a feeling of stunning self-worth. Tuning in to this internalized sense of self-worth creates positive imprints on the mind which will, over time, enable you to develop positive expectations that help you attract success luck, making you a winner and helping you achieve the things you set out to do.

Winning is an attitude and a mind set. But winning also requires luck: being at the right place at the right time, meeting someone special, having an opportunity thrown your way and getting a small but vital edge within a competitive environment. Feng shui can provide this bit of luck to give you the necessary boost to tip results in your favour. Often this bit of luck can mean the difference between getting the job or scholarship you were after, or the raise you wanted so badly. Remember, this is a very competitive world that is becoming even more so and we need all the luck we can get.

To make the best use of feng shui, however, you must start by seeing real value in yourself. You must accept yourself and your life situation unconditionally. Only then can you focus clearly on the things you need to achieve to raise your self-worth and value. If you want an abundance of attainments and achievements you must embrace the person you are. Discard feelings of unwarranted inferiority. Clear out fears of unworthiness, shrug off insecurities and reject defensive behaviour.

And from this moment stop telling yourself how difficult it is to learn feng shui. See it as an additional subject you can easily master. Like a school subject. See it as a tool, as something you can use for the rest of your life and worth learning. See it as a piece of knowledge that will make you so helpful to all friends and relatives.

Take a relaxed attitude towards feng shui and towards your efforts to improve yourself and your circumstance. You must believe you can learn anything, and that you can do anything if you put your heart into it. You must refuse to feel defeated by small obstacles. All of this requires an attitude transformation and a mental re-programming which you can practise in tandem with feng shui, often with amazing results. This was what I did for over 15 years.

I built up confidence by progressively programming myself. I used to meditate on the things I was good at, my strengths and the skills I had, or needed to acquire. It is easy to feel confident in something one is already good at, or at an expertise that one has trained for and is thus competent at doing. But the business of living requires an infinite amount of knowledge and know-how that can sometimes put huge dents in our self-confidence. This was how I felt when I first started learning to do my own feng shui, which also coincided with my climb up the career ladder. It would have been foolish had I allowed any feeling of inadequacy to immobilize me.

I was not completely confident, but I always ignored little hiccups along the way. Adopting this approach allowed me to focus on what I needed to go after in order to grow, both as a professional and as a person. This was the motivation that led me to improve my paper qualifications. I applied to do my MBA at the Harvard Business School using my determination to get the much-needed admission. Then I used feng shui to get me the money to go to business school. I moved my bed to align my sleeping direction so that I could receive good fortune and success chi from my best direction. The method did not fail me and I succeeded in getting a United Nations fellowship to attend business school.

Over time, I saw positive results from doing my own feng shui, so that all through my corporate career days I used my knowledge of feng shui as an additional management tool. There were, of course, moments when I was so carried away by my work that I forgot about feng shui. During those months I suffered from quite severe bad luck. Fortunately for me, I always realized in time and corrected the situation. Feng shui has thus been a good friend for many years now.

I am writing this book to tell you and everyone else that you can do it too. There is nothing mysterious or very spiritual about feng shui. I have never treated feng shui as a paranormal or spiritual method of making magic. It really is a method of harnessing good energies and dissolving bad energies, and once you understand how to practise it, you will be able to protect yourself from bad feng shui; and enhance any space to benefit from good feng shui. You do not need any special spiritual or psychic powers to do this. But you can use the power of your mind to strengthen feng shui methods and techniques you have learnt and implemented.

Improving oneself is, of course, a never-ending quest. It always feels good when you successfully acquire new knowledge, new experiences, new abilities and new qualifications. No matter what stage of life you are at, and how old you are, personal growth creates a special sense of abundance. You can develop it into a successful habit, so that feeling good about yourself becomes a part of you with no problem. At the same time you can let something else become a habit. You can let feng shui become a habit.

Let feng shui be a lifelong friend so that seeing with feng shui eyes becomes second nature to you. This does not mean becoming addicted to feng shui but it does require a heightening of your awareness of its existence. Learn feng shui as a means of understanding the energies in your environment. But do not allow it to rule you.

Energizing your personal chi energy

Advanced feng shui practitioners possess secret methods that enable them to harness a great deal of personal chi which they use to enter into a meditative state for special feng shui consultations. These methods vary from master to master and from what I have seen, they tend to be more shamanic techniques than feng shui. Some of these secret methods have been passed to me but I have found it quite unnecessary to depend on them. It is sufficient to use simple landscape and compass formula feng shui and then to combine that with my own mind-enhancing techniques. This may be considered secret, but I am happy indeed to present them here in this book.

Let me start by sharing a couple of very simple yet very special chi kung exercises (see box, below) which you can learn to raise the chi within you. Chi kung is a form of exercise that allows you to use your own personal chi to develop a healthy body. These methods manifest the physical chi in that you can feel the energy move inside you. It is not necessary for you to learn chi kung to benefit from feng shui. But you should try to feel this chi that is personal to you, that belongs to you. Only then can you really tune into your own force field and the cosmic breath that lies within you. Only then can you visualize aligning it with the cosmic energies of the living space around you.

Exercises to access your personal chi

1 Stand with feet about 45 cm (18 in) apart. Bend down slightly but keep your back very straight. Do not lean over. Keeping the back straight is part of the secret of chi kung and kung fu methods to raise the chi in martial fighters. Next extend your arms to the side of you so that your body resembles a cross. Now flex the fingers of your hands upwards such that your hands are at a 90-degrees angle to your arm. Hold this pose for about ten minutes. You will feel the chi starting to move on the palms of your hand and slowly making its way up your hands and into your body. If you do this exercise daily, inside of a month you will be able to feel, control and even manipulate the flow of this chi energy between your hands. But that will be all you can do. Please do not run away with the notion that this simple exercise is all there is to chi kung. It merely lets you feel your chi, and

is good for helping you energize objects with your personal chi, but it certainly does not make you a chi kung expert. Chi kung itself is a wonderful science that has to be learnt separately.

2 Stand with your feet 45 cm (18 in) apart and with your back straight, lower your body a little way. This engages the largest muscle in your body and in the early days of doing this exercise your upper legs will ache. It is also a very good way of losing inches! Now bring your hands in front of you with the palms facing each other as if you are holding a small live bird. Tune in to the imaginary bird between your hands and gently move your hands together and apart very slightly. Slowly your palms heat up and you will feel the energy that is trapped between them. Imagine this energy as a sphere of light which expands and contracts according to your mental instructions.

Using quartz crystal to improve exam results

Sensing your own intrinsic energy is the starting point for energizing your personal chi. When you are sufficiently warmed up through doing one or both of the exercises opposite, you should place your hands around a cluster of natural quartz crystal or a round crystal ball which you will need to purchase specially for this purpose. Then place the crystal globe on a table in the northeast corner of your living room or study. This will bring wonderful earth luck to all your endeavours at improving yourself. This technique is particularly helpful for households with school or college children since energizing the northeast corner in this way generally brings wonderful luck for the attainment of educational achievement.

Let each child have his/her own crystal which may be a crystal cluster or a round crystal ball. Let each of them warm up their hands internally as described and then feel the crystal so that their energies have been efficiently passed on to the crystal. Then place the crystal on a table in the northeast corner of the living room. You can also place the crystal on a table in the northeast of their respective bedrooms.

This method of energizing for good exam results works by making the child more focused, improves their concentration and makes them highly motivated. It is a good idea to enhance the energies of the crystal regularly by holding the crystal and allowing it to absorb the personal energies of the child concerned. Do not let anyone else touch these crystals. This is because you would not want different energies to be stored in the crystal. Foreign energies may well be negative or may clash badly with those of your child, so guard your energizing crystals carefully.

For the same reason, before you use any crystal for feng shui purposes, it is a good idea to cleanse the crystal of lingering alien and foreign energies. When they are in shop windows and cupboards and handled by so many strangers, crystals pick up other people's vibrations. To remove these energies, fill the bowl to its brim with water and then dissolve 7 tablespoons of sea salt in the water. Soak the crystal for seven days and nights in the bowl and after that place it under running tap water. This effectively removes all other energies. You can then charge the crystal with your energy or with the energy of the person whose educational luck you want to energize.

A lapis lazuli globe

An even more effective way of energizing education luck for children is to place a real globe in the northeast corner. This can be a globe of the earth rotating on its axis or better yet it can be a specially designed globe made of crystal, lapis lazuli or topaz. These latter objects are quite expensive but they are also create extremely good feng shui for the great good fortune of achieving high honours in education.

The globe is a superb symbol of the earth, and placing it in the northeast, which represents the educational aspirations of the family, is a very efficient way of activating the earth element of the northeast. My personal preference is a globe made of lapis lazuli which I used with enormous success for my daughter all through her school and university years. If you cannot find such a globe, you can also use one made of crystal.

Do not forget to let the child hold the globe after raising his/her chi energy with the exercises. It is important that the relevant personal energy of the person who wishes to benefit from the energizer be passed on to the crystal.

Aligning personal chi with space chi

In addition to the above techniques that combine symbolic feng shui with the five element theory of feng shui, you can also use the eight mansions formula which categorizes people into east and west groups. I call this the Pa Kua Lo Shu formula. It is a very powerful compass formula taken from the classical texts for determining the most auspicious directions and locations according to birth dates and gender. The formula offers a personalized method of determining auspicious and inauspicious alignments between the personal chi of the individual resident and the space chi of the environment. The formula is very easy to apply but there are many different ways of using it. Indeed, I have written an entire book on this formula alone because there are simply so many applications and so much feng shui relevance to the formula. Many different applications of the formula are dealt with throughout this book wherever it becomes relevant to the kind of abundance we wish to actualize.

Kua numbers determined by the Chinese lunar calendar

To obtain your Kua number, you need to first determine your year of birth according to the lunar calendar. You get this by noting the cut off dates for each new year. Thus, if you were born on 5 Feb 1975, your year of birth is *not* 1975 but is instead 1974. Again, if you were born on 21 Jan 1987, then your lunar year of birth is not 1987 but is 1986. Your Kua number is also given here. If you want to know how these numbers are derived, see the formula on page 62.

ANIMAL (element)	Male Kua number	Female Kua number	WESTERN CALENDAR DATES	YEAR ELEMENT
Rat (water)	7	8	18 Feb 1912 – 5 Feb 1913	Water
Ox (earth)	6	9	6 Feb 1913 – 25 Jan 1914	Water
Tiger (wood)	5	1	26 Jan 1914 – 13 Feb 1915	Wood
Rabbit (wood)	4	2	14 Feb 1915 – 2 Feb 1916	Wood
Dragon (earth)	3	3	3 Feb 1916 – 22 Jan 1917	Fire
Snake (fire)	2	4	23 Jan 1917 – 10 Feb 1918	Fire
Horse (fire)	1	5	11 Feb 1918 – 31 Jan 1919	Earth
Sheep (earth)	9	6	1 Feb 1919 – 19 Feb 1920	Earth
Monkey (metal)	8	7	20 Feb 1920 – 7 Feb 1921	Metal
Rooster (metal)	7	8	8 Feb 1921 – 27 Jan 1922	Metal
Dog (earth)	6	9	28 Jan 1922 – 15 Feb 1923	Water
Boar (water)	5	1	16 Feb 1923 – 4 Feb 1924	Water
J start of 60 year cycle				
Rat (water)	4	2	5 Feb 1924 – 23 Jan 1925	Wood
Ox (earth)	3	3	24 Jan 1925 – 12 Feb 1926	Wood
Tiger (wood)	2	4	13 Feb 1926 – 1 Feb 1927	Fre
Rabbit (wood)	1	5	2 Feb 1927 – 22 Jan 1928	Fire
Dragon (earth)	9	6	23 Jan 1928 – 9 Feb 1929	Earth
Snake (fire)	8	7	10 Feb 1929 – 29 Jan 1930	Earth
Horse (fire)	7	8	30 Jan 1930 – 16 Feb 1931	Metal
Sheep (earth)	6	9	17 Feb 1931 – 5 Feb 1932	Metal
Monkey (metal)	5	1	6 Feb 1932 – 25 Jan 1933	Water
Rooster (metal)	4	2	26 Jan 1933 – 13 Feb 1934	Water
Dog (earth)	3	3	14 Feb 1934 – 3 Feb 1935	Wood
Boar (water)	2	4	4 Feb 1935 – 23 Jan 1936	Wood
Rat (water)	1	5	24 Jan 1936 – 10 Feb 1937	Fire
Ox (earth)	9	6	11 Feb 1937 – 30 Jan 1938	Fire

ANIMAL (element)	Male Kua number	Female Kua number	WESTERN CALENDAR DATES	YEAR ELEMENT
Tiger (wood)	8	7	31 Jan 1938 – 18 Feb 1939	Earth
Rabbit (wood)	7	8	19 Feb 1939 – 7 Feb 1940	Earth
Dragon (earth)	6	9	8 Feb 1940 – 26 Jan 1941	Metal
Snake (fire)	5	1	27 Jan 1941 – 14 Feb 1942	Metal
Horse (fire)	4	2	15 Feb 1942 – 4 Feb 1943	Water
Sheep (earth)	3	3	5 Feb 1943 – 24 Jan 1944	Water
Monkey (metal)	2	4	25 Jan 1944 – 12 Feb 1945	Wood
Rooster (metal)	1	5	13 Feb 1945 – 1 Feb 1946	Wood
Dog (earth)	9	6	2 Feb 1946 – 21 Jan 1947	Fire
Boar (water)	8	7	22 Jan 1947 – 9 Feb 1948	Fire
Rat (water)	7	8	10 Feb 1948 – 28 Jan 1949	Earth
Ox (earth)	6	9	29 Jan 1949 – 16 Feb 1950	Earth
Tiger (wood)	5	1	17 Feb 1950 – 5 Feb 1951	Metal
Rabbit (wood)	4	2	6 Feb 1951 – 26 Jan 1952	Metal
Dragon (earth)	3	3	27 Jan 1952 – 13 Feb 1953	Water
Snake (fire)	2	4	14 Feb 1953 – 2 Feb 1954	Water
Horse (fire)	1	5	3 Feb 1954 – 23 Jan 1955	Wood
Sheep (earth)	9	6	24 Jan 1955 – 11 Feb 1956	Wood
Monkey (metal)	8	7	12 Feb 1956 – 30 Jan 1957	Fire
Rooster (metal)	7	8	31 Jan 1957 – 17 Feb 1958	Fire
Dog (earth)	6	9	18 Feb 1958 – 7 Feb 1959	Earth
Boar (water)	5	1	8 Feb 1959 – 27 Jan 1960	Earth
Rat (water)	4	2	28 Jan 1960 – 14 Feb 1961	Metal
Ox (earth)	3	3	15 Feb 1961 – 4 Feb 1962	Metal
Tiger (wood)	2	4	5 Feb 1962 – 24 Jan 1963	Water
Rabbit (wood)	1	5	25 Jan 1963 – 12 Feb 1964	Water
Dragon (earth)	9	6	13 Feb 1964 – 1 Feb 1965	Wood
Snake (fire)	8	7	2 Feb 1965 – 20 Jan 1966	Wood
Horse (fire)	7	8	21 Jan 1966 – 8 Feb 1967	Fire
Sheep (earth)	6	9	9 Feb 1967 – 29 Jan 1968	Fire
Monkey (metal)	5	1	30 Jan 1968 – 16 Feb 1969	Earth
Rooster (metal)	4	2	17 Feb 1969 – 5 Feb 1970	Earth
Dog (earth)	3	3	6 Feb 1970 – 26 Jan 1971	Metal
Boar (water)	2	4	27 Jan 1971 – 14 Feb 1972	Metal
Rat (water)	1	5	15 Feb 1972 – 2 Feb 1973	Water
Ox (earth)	9	6	3 Feb 1973 – 22 Jan 1974	Water

ANIMAL (element)	Male Kua number	Female Kua number	WESTERN CALENDAR DATES	YEAR ELEMENT
Tiger (wood)	8	7	23 Jan 1974 – 10 Feb 1975	Wood
Rabbit (wood)	7	8	11 Feb 1975 – 30 Jan 1976	Wood
Dragon (earth)	6	9	31 Jan 1976 – 17 Feb 1977	Fire
Snake (fire)	5	1	18 Feb 1977 – 6 Feb 1978	Fire
Horse (fire)	4	2	7 Feb 1978 – 27 Jan 1979	Earth
Sheep (earth)	3	3	28 Jan 1979 – 15 Feb 1980	Earth
Monkey (metal)	2	4	16 Feb 1980 – 4 Feb 1981	Metal
Rooster (metal)	1	5	5 Feb 1981 – 24 Jan 1982	Metal
Dog (earth)	9	6	25 Jan 1982 – 12 Feb 1983	Water
Boar (water)	8	7	13 Feb 1983 – 1 Feb 1984	Water
Rat (water)	7	8	2 Feb 1984 – 19 Feb 1985	Wood
Ox (earth)	6	9	20 Feb 1985 – 8 Feb 1986	Wood
Tiger (wood)	5	1	9 Feb 1986 – 28 Jan 1987	Fire
Rabbit (wood)	4	2	29 Jan 1987 – 16 Feb 1988	Fire
Dragon (earth)	3	3	17 Feb 1988 – 5 Feb 1989	Earth
Snake (fire)	2	4	6 Feb 1989 – 26 Jan 1990	Earth
Horse (fire)	1	5	27 Jan 1990 – 14 Feb 1991	Metal
Sheep (earth)	9	6	15 Feb 1991 – 3 Feb 1992	Metal
Monkey (metal)	8	7	4 Feb 1992 – 22 Jan 1993	Water
Rooster (metal)	7	8	23 Jan 1993 – 9 Feb 1994	Water
Dog (earth)	6	9	10 Feb 1994 – 30 Jan 1995	Wood
Boar (water)	5	1	31 Jan 1995 – 18 Feb 1996	Wood
Rat (water)	4	2	19 Feb 1996 – 6 Feb 1997	Fire
Ox (earth)	3	3	7 Feb 1997 – 27 Jan 1998	Fire
Tiger (wood)	2	4	28 Jan 1998 – 15 Feb 1999	Earth
Rabbit (wood)	1	5	16 Feb 1999 – 4 Feb 2000	Earth
Dragon (earth)	9	6	5 Feb 2000 – 23 Jan 2001	Metal
Snake (fire)	8	7	24 Jan 2001 – 11 Feb 2002	Metal
Horse (fire)	7	8	12 Feb 2002 – 31 Jan 2003	Water
Sheep (earth)	6	9	1 Feb 2003 – 21 Jan 2004	Water
Monkey (metal)	5	1	22 Jan 2004 – 8 Feb 2005	Wood
Rooster (metal)	4	2	9 Feb 2005 – 28 Jan 2006	Wood
Dog (earth)	3	3	29 Jan 2006 – 17 Feb 2007	Fire
Boar (water)	2	4	18 Feb 2007 – 6 Feb 2008	Fire

The Pa Kua Lo Shu formula

To determine your personal auspicious and inauspicious directions, you must first work out your personal Kua number. The calculation of this personal Kua number requires your lunar year of birth and your gender. The lunar year of birth can only be determined if you know the date of your birth as well. Check against the table of lunar years reproduced on pages 59–61 and use the method described in the box below to work out your Kua number.

With your Kua number you will be able to determine several things:

1 If you belong to the east or west group directions
2 Your four auspicious directions
3 Your four inauspicious directions
4 Your best personal growth direction
5 Your success direction
6 Your best health direction
7 Your best marriage direction
8 The part of your house to avoid
9 The part of your house that brings you the greatest luck.

The above are some of the uses of the Kua number and the more important and effective techniques of using the formula will be dealt with throughout the book.

Determining your Kua number

For men

Take your lunar year of birth
Add the last two digits
Reduce to a single number
Deduct from 10

Example 1: Year of birth 1964
6+4=10 and 1+0=1
10-1= 9
The Kua number is 9.

Example 2: Year of birth 1984
8+4=12 and 1+2=3
10-3 = 7
The Kua is 7.

For women

Take the lunar year of birth
Add the last two digits
Reduce to a single number and add 5
If the result is more than ten reduce to a single digit.

Example 1: Year of birth 1945
4+5=9 and 9+5=14
1+4=5
The Kua number is 5.

Example 2: Year of birth 1982
8+2=10 and 1+0=1
1+5=6
The Kua number is 6.

East and west groups

- East group people have the Kua numbers 1,3,4 and 9 and their four auspicious directions are north, south, southeast and east. These are the east group directions and any one of these directions will bring good luck to people belonging to this group.
- West group people have Kua numbers 2,5,6,7 and 8 and for this group the four auspicious directions are west, southwest, northwest and northeast. If you are a west group person any one of these directions will bring you good fortune.
- Note that east group directions are inauspicious for west group people and vice versa. Try to memorize your Kua number and also your directions so you will always know your good and bad directions in any situation. Have a compass handy and you can practise this simple feng shui technique wherever you are.

East and west group people

This formula maintains that everyone is either east group or west group. Generally, people of the same group tend to be more compatible. East group people get along better with other east group people and the same is true of west group people. To find out if you are an east group or west group person check the table above.

Energizing for personal growth

The most effective way to activate your personal growth luck is to use the Pa Kua Lo Shu formula. To discover your most auspicious personalized direction – the direction that will do the most to enhance your development as a person – take your Kua number and refer to the Pa Kua of the Later Heaven Arrangement (the yang Pa Kua) to determine the corresponding compass direction of your Kua number. For ease of reference the table left summarizes this.

By referring to the table you will be able to identify the most important direction and corner within your home in terms of your personal fulfilment luck. This is the feeling of abundance that accompanies the attainment of significant improvements to your credentials, professional or educational endeavours. If you are a student, energizing this direction will help you to study better, have improved concentration and study skills and most importantly imbue you with very strong motivation to do well.

Most auspicious growth and development directions

Your Kua number	Direction
1	north
2	southwest
3	east
4	southeast
5	southwest for men, northeast for women
6	northwest
7	west
8	northeast
9	south

The application techniques

1 Sit at your desk facing your direction. If it is east then the compass in front of you should be pointing east. You must try to be very accurate, and I recommend people to actually draw out an arrow on their desk so that they are reminded of the most beneficial direction. Try to tap this best direction when you study, when you do your homework and also when you take your exams. If you cannot, make sure that you at least sit facing one of your other auspicious directions.

2 Sleep on your bed with your head pointing in the direction that is the best for you. This will ensure that in addition to energizing for personal growth at your desk during the hours of daylight, you are continuing to energize it during your nocturnal hours of sleep as well. This means that the head end of the bed must be orientated to this direction.

3 Orientate to face this best direction whenever you meet anyone for an important interview. Indeed, if you are facing your own good direction and the person opposite you happens (by sheer bad luck) to be facing his worst direction, you will be able to get whatever you want out of the interview. Again, you can only do this if you carry a pocket compass wherever you go.

If you are already working, energizing this direction will help you to gain greater confidence in yourself and open up opportunities for you to enhance your professional qualifications. For those engaged in any kind of study this is the direction that will enable you to directly align your own personal flow of chi with that of the environment.

This personal growth direction is also the best direction to face for meditation. It will bring you results much faster and enable you to concentrate better. The way this works is that by facing your personal growth direction, the energies coming from that direction will be the most auspicious for you.

Additional methods of enhancing each direction

It is also good to add another dimension to the energizing technique being used. Do this by applying the five element theory: identify which element is represented by your most auspicious direction and then hang an object that symbolizes the element that is most helpful to your element. The relevant elements and suggested symbolic objects are given here as suggestions only. You can also use your own creativity once you understand the fundamentals of the practice.

If your direction is west or northwest

The element to energize is metal. Which element produces metal? Earth produces metal, so from where you are sitting place objects that represent the earth element to face you. This will symbolically produce the element that will energize your luck. Earth objects are anything made of stone, ceramic, glass, crystal, clay or sand. An excellent suggestion is the use of crystal or a porcelain vase. Place it just about 3 m (10 ft) in front of you. If you like, you can also use a painting of an earth element object like a small hillock for instance. Do not hang a picture of a mountain in front of you even though it represents the earth. When you sit facing a mountain it is like confronting it and this is inauspicious. It is necessary to stay balanced. Avoid having anything that belongs to the fire element.

If your direction is east, or southeast

The element to energize will be wood. The element that produces wood is water, and as such placing a water feature in front of where you sit will be excellent. This water feature can be something as simple as an urn of water. Or it can be an aquarium or a fountain. For personal growth, however, usually a painting of a water scene is sufficient since water is best used for energizing wealth luck rather than the luck of personal growth. Having said that, using water is always auspicious when used correctly. Avoid having anything of the metal element.

If your direction is southwest or northeast

The element you need to energize will be the fire element. Place something red directly facing you like a painting whose dominant colours are red. Or hang curtains that are red in colour or hang a bright light. In the cycle of elements, fire produces the earth element of the southwest and northeast. It is also lucky to place objects that suggest the earth element since earth luck is particularly auspicious in these two sectors. Avoid having anything that suggests the water element because water destroys earth.

If your direction is north

The element you need to energize is water. Here the compatible and producing element is metal. Place anything that is made of metal (or gold would be even better) in front of you – a Hi-Fi set, a wall clock, tinkling wind chimes to enhance the energies that are coming from the north. It will bring great good fortune to you in the form of huge success in all your endeavours.

If your direction is south

The element you will have to energize will be fire, in which case having a plant directly in front of you will be most auspicious. Make sure the plant looks healthy and verdant. It is also a good idea to use a flowering plant since this suggests that you are starting to blossom. The Chinese believe that the scholar's luck starts to bloom just as he is about to qualify with high honours at the Imperial exams. This can be compared to college and university exams of today.

Creating a private sanctuary

When you have identified your direction and the element that is best for you, it is a good idea to consider building a private sanctuary within your home that is meant exclusively for you. You should decorate this sanctuary in a most auspicious way and this means aligning your personal chi with the chi of your environment so that the energy flow in the sanctuary is both harmonious and balanced. It should also be conducive to your efforts at thinking, meditating and being creative. Follow these guidelines when creating your sanctuary.

1 Select a part of your home that coincides with the direction that is best for your personal development. Use your Kua number to identify this direction and use a compass placed in the centre of your apartment to point out this most suitable location.

2 Identify the element of that corner. If a storeroom, a toilet or the kitchen already occupies this part of the house, it suggests a certain amount of negative effect on your personal development luck. But you can, if you so wish, go to the living room or bedroom and identify the corner of that room that corresponds to your best personal development direction. Your sanctuary can thus be a special corner in either of these rooms.

3 Mark out the space and energize it with one of the purification exercises given in the last chapter (pages 49–51) using either incense or tinkling bells. Clear the energy carefully so that all lingering remains of past activities are symbolically purified.

4 Decorate the corner in colours that are harmonious with the element of the corner. These colours can be reflected as colours on the wall, curtains, carpets and scatter cushions. As a quick guide note that:
   ◆ all shades of red represent the fire element and are suitable for the south, southwest and northeast
   ◆ all shades of green and brown represent the wood element and are suitable for the east, southeast and south
   ◆ all shades of black and blue represent the element water and are suitable for the north, east and southeast
   ◆ all shades of white and metallic colours represent the metal element and are suitable for the west, northwest and north
   ◆ all shades of ochre represent earth and are suitable for the southwest, northeast, west and northwest.

5 Finally, energize the corner by placing an object there that symbolizes the element of that corner. In the west and northwest you may wish to place a metal bell or wind chime. In the southwest or northeast you may wish to hang a crystal; in the south hang a bright light, in the southeast and east place healthy growing plants, and in the north place a small water feature.

As far as possible you should use your private sanctuary as just that – a sanctuary where you will do your best thinking. This should also be the place for you to study and meditate. Sit facing your best direction to receive excellent energies.

Breaking the barriers of self

Do not do any of the above if you feel sceptical or doubtful. While you do not need to believe in feng shui for it to work, if you have any doubts you will unknowingly be empowering your space with negative energies. The mind truly is all-powerful and if you shoot out disbelief and scepticism these act like invisible poison arrows that slice into the effectiveness of all that you may have done to alleviate the energies of the space. They send out killing chi that work strongly against the harmony that has been created. Remember that feng shui is all about the manipulation of energies within your living space and there is no greater source of positive or negative energy than you yourself.

Human beings exude huge amounts of chi that have a great effect on their own environment. It is therefore advisable for you to work at breaking the barriers of the self before you proceed any further. If you are not convinced about feng shui's effectiveness, it is better to stick to the simple energizing techniques first. See feng shui at work and feel the lightness of a space which has good feng shui before embarking on something as advanced as building a private feng shui sanctuary.

Breaking the barriers of self require you to use your own intellect to logically think through the practice of feng shui. Be relaxed about your scepticism. You do not need to have faith in feng shui. It is not a religion. But you should be convinced that it is something worth putting into practice. Better to hold an indifferent attitude than to be tense about it. Feng shui cannot make you win the lottery instantly, or bring you success overnight. So it is not something you should become all tensed up about. It is foolish to blame every piece of bad luck on bad feng shui just as it is ridiculous to give feng shui credit for every piece of good fortune. Remember that feng shui accounts for only one third of your luck.

Look on feng shui luck as a strategic stake in your destiny that is within your control. Build your space according to its guidelines and then sit back, expectant of the success luck that will come to you. Forget what you have done to energize your feng shui. Simply relax and move on . . . and a year later take stock of whether you have grown as a person and whether you feel better. If it was an exam year, see if your grades have improved. And if it was a professionally crucial year, see if the year has brought positive changes.

When you are satisfied that you do see tangible and discernible results you can move on to more advanced methods that bring even greater success and happiness. This is the way to break the negative energies that are inadvertently created by the self.

Dissolving the blockages in your space

There are blockages in the space around you which are created by three tangible and intangible forces. These are:

- the forces of material physical objects and structures,
- the forces of sounds and speech and
- the forces of the mind.

The forces created by physical objects are the easiest to deal with since these can be moved and re-arranged to allow the energies to flow in a harmonious and auspicious way. The rule of thumb is that energies should be made to flow slowly, and in a gently curving way. Energies should never flow straight and fast. Large pieces of furniture, pillars and beams should also not appear threatening and imposing. This creates a feeling of hostility, which causes chi to become petrified and blocked.

Let the flow of movement within the home stay clear of protruding sharp corners and heavy, exposed, overhead beams. If there is a pillar seemingly blocking the flow, either soften its edges with plants or wrap it with mirrors to symbolically make it disappear.

If there is clutter blocking the flow of chi, clear it. If there is too much furniture give some away. When furniture seems wobbly and the hinges spoilt, get them all repaired as soon as you can. When the bulbs have blown, change them. When drains get blocked, bring in the plumber. Let the flow of the home be smooth at all times. This is the secret of feng shui.

4 An abundance of acclaim

'What use is there of
success, wealth and power . . .
When one's life is
Totally devoid of honour.

A good name
Is what brings acclaim

It is what makes
The superior human being.'

ACCORDING to Chinese tradition, life is devoid of meaning when you do not have a good name. The most precious manifestation of abundance is to possess a reputation that is honourable and highly respected. This is the abundance of acclaim that is considered central to real and meaningful success. Feng shui directly addresses this in its categorization of the eight types of luck that define the aspirations of mankind.

If a person comes from a family whose name is respected far and wide, and whose patriarch is looked up to by society as someone of sterling reputation, that person is said to possess great good fortune. All the great classics of China, and especially the great Book of Changes, the *I Ching*, frequently refer to the superior man throughout its pages, as if to suggest that the only way to be is to build a reputation for being honourable, upright and honest. This brings the great good fortune of widespread acclaim that creates its own brand of stunning abundance. Money alone is worthless without a good name and all of the other aspirations of life – health, family, success and so forth – also seem empty without the abundance that comes with a good name.

It is therefore not surprising that one of the most vital manifestations of luck that feng shui focuses on is the luck of critical acclaim and the attainment of a good reputation. This requires activating the energies that enhance recognition of your credentials and attributes. Good fortune chi is manipulated to create general awareness and recognition of your good qualities. This brings you the respect of your peers and colleagues that ultimately lead to widespread fame and fortune.

This kind of luck is especially required by those in the entertainment and political professions – singers, dancers, politicians and actors all need to energize this kind of feng shui luck. Professionals in the corporate environment also need the luck of acclaim. In business today, reputation is everything. Unless you are recognized as an upright person in society it is difficult indeed for other forms of success and aspirations to be realized. People simply will not do business with those who do not have a good name.

Recognition is the underlying requirement of success. There are so many people who are as talented, work as hard as and even have better credentials than their counterparts who make it big! What differentiates the very successful from the moderately successful and the moderately successful from the unsuccessful, even though all have the same abilities and work just as hard, is the luck of recognition. The winner always has two things working in his/her favour – one will be a level of determination to gain recognition that is so extremely pronounced, the mind sends out positive energies that attract success. This represents the harnessing of mankind luck.

The other factor is the possession of good feng shui by harnessing the luck of the earth to provide for that extra intangible advantage. Sometimes, recognition luck has been harnessed even without you knowing it. Simply by having a very bright light in the correct corner of the office or home, for example, will energize the luck of recognition.

Many talented people shrivel into obscurity because nobody discovered them or acknowledged their talents sufficiently to give them a chance. This applies to all and every profession. The more recognized a person is, and the more respect he or she garners, the higher will be his/her chances of success. It is for this reason that the Chinese always refer to anyone who is perceived to be hugely successful as someone who enjoys the great abundance of having a very yang life. This has its roots in the belief that it is the precious yang energy of both the person and the environment, which propel men and women to heights of recognizable achievements.

This refers to the bright and alive side of the yin and yang cosmology that is believed to express the totality of the Universe. Yin and yang are two poles of the cosmic spectrum of existence. The energies of yin and yang are opposites but they are not opposing. They are complementary, one giving existence to the other. Yin describes the sombre moods of life and symbolizes inactivity and death while yang signifies the brightness of life, activity and growth. Yang is said to be vibrant and warm, and the mood of yang eloquently symbolizes all that is abundant and energetic about life.

Having a yang life suggests a life of great abundance, and houses of the living are described as yang houses. Good feng shui creates an optimum balance of yin and yang which, in houses of the living, suggest the need for a greater dose of yang than yin. But yin should never be overshadowed to an extent that it becomes completely absent. When yin ceases to exist altogether, yang too is said to disintegrate because one gives existence to the other. The nuance of the yin and yang cosmology is thus a fine line that requires delicate balancing. It is important to have the presence of strong yang energy, but at all times you must ensure that yin energy is also present.

Activating the luck of reputation

The feng shui of recognition luck requires an abundance of yang energy that can be created in several different ways. Yang energy is not difficult to produce and it is generally associated with two main techniques: the use of the fire element particularly red, and the energizing of the south corner of the room.

Based on the Later Heaven Arrangement of the Pa Kua, the trigram associated with recognition, respect and fame is that of *li*. It signifies the element of fire and is placed south in the yang Pa Kua. Translated into feng shui terms, it is the south part of any home that best represents reputation and fame. If this corner of the house is arranged to have good feng shui, the patriarch of the house (as well as the entire family) will benefit from excellent reputation luck that brings great honours and accolades.

The fame trigram

The fame and acclaim trigram is the trigram *li* which is made up of one broken yin line sandwiched between two unbroken solid lines. This trigram appears strong on the outside but soft and vulnerable on the inside, expressing the tenuous nature of mankind's reputation. However, *li* symbolizes the brightness of fire as well as the dazzle of the sun. It represents the glory and adulation and applause of the masses. It also symbolizes heat and activity. The meaning of this trigram is that of a great person who perpetuates the light by rising to prominence. The person's name and fame will illuminate the four corners of the universe, dazzling everyone with exemplary achievements and attainments.

At its ultimate, this trigram also symbolizes lightning and this gives an idea of the intrinsic and fleeting brilliance it stands for. To activate this trigram in the south wall of your home, you can incorporate its three lined sequence into ceiling designs, door designs and furniture decorations.

The way to activate the feng shui of good reputation is to invest in a beautiful crystal chandelier and hang it in the south. This is the most effective feng shui energizer for creating the abundance of acclaim. Indeed, when the light is kept on for the better part of the day and night, this energizer will bring more than simply a good reputation. It brings fame and fortune as well, thereby creating an abundance of critical acclaim that will bring benefits for all the residents. Yes, keep the chandelier turned on even during the hours of daylight. This creates very powerful yang energy which in turn attracts wonderful good fortune into the household. Do not worry about the cost of electricity. The success luck, which the chandelier's light will bring you, will be more than sufficient to cover the cost of keeping the light switched on.

A second way of energizing for the luck of reputation is to paint this part of the house a very bright red. If your study is located in the south for instance, it is not a bad idea to paint the walls of the room a bright vermilion red. Red is a very powerful yang colour that is always associated with good reputation luck. If you don't like your room to be red, you can opt to paint only the door into your study a bright or a maroon red. It may sound a little drastic and loud but after you have done it, you will be amazed at the rush of energy that enfolds you. This is the yang energy stirring your senses.

To augment this feeling you can also hang a fake firecracker – the kind which the Chinese hang on their doorways during the lunar New Year – to symbolically create a lot of noise. The firecracker is a very yang symbol. A loud sound is always associated with the clap of thunder analogous with the rise of a person to prominence. As such, this is an excellent energizer to actively create the luck of acclaim.

And, finally, if all of these things are beyond your reach, you can also hang a picture or painting of a sunrise, or of sunflowers in full bloom. This latter recommendation must be implemented with care since sunflowers blooming suggest abundance while sunflowers drooping suggest a reputation that is fading. In the same way, displaying fresh flowers in the south is also very yang but once the flowers fade they become yin and must be thrown out. In view of this, it is easier to have a painting of flowers or to use fake flowers. Having said this, the real thing is always better. You just need to be diligent about changing the water and the flowers when they fade.

Counteracting poor feng shui

If the south corner has poor feng shui, bad luck will prevail and the residents of the house will find it tough to command the respect of peers. People will look down on them no matter how hard they try to gain respect. Sometimes, when the feng shui of this corner is seriously afflicted, the family patriarch could very well suffer from severe damage to his reputation such as being trapped in scandal, or worse, being convicted of felonies thereby bringing disgrace to the family name. Generally, an afflicted south corner causes enemies to bad mouth the family. There is thus a general air of bad feeling.

A south corner is said to be seriously afflicted when the corner is overwhelmed by yin energies and is being hit by severe shar chi or killing breath. Excessive yin energy in the south is caused by the presence of too many water element symbols. For example, when there is a preponderance of the colours blue and black to the exclusion of yang colours the energy is said to be very yin. If the space is cramped, yin energies also prevail over yang energies. And when there is the presence of a toilet that is frequently used, the luck of the south is afflicted. If simultaneously the family patriarch has his bedroom in the south, bad luck associated with his reputation will result. This can be manifested mildly, simply as having a reputation for being difficult or stubborn or being hard to work with; or the actualization of the bad luck can be more severe.

How the bad luck manifests itself depends also on other factors, including the patriarch's own heaven luck, his astrological chart as well as the family's collective heaven luck. The Buddhists also believe in karma and when severe ill-fortune occurs, especially ill-fortune associated with the collapse of one's name, it is regarded as the ripening of negative karma.

Killing breath or shar chi is caused by the presence of poison arrows inside the house, and in particular in the south corner of the house. This can be due to a variety of features but the most common are the sharp edges of protruding corners, stand-alone pillars and the edges of walls. Poison arrows are also caused by the presence of a flow of energy that is straight and threatening such as the presence of three doors in a row or a long corridor leading to the south corner. Unless these feng shui afflictions are corrected by slowing down the fast flow of energy, the south corner could well suffer from the affliction. Usually, using plants and wind chimes to slow down the energy and soften the edges of corners are very effective ways of diffusing killing energy. When using plants, place them against the edge of corners and pillars to soften these edges. This will cause the plant to absorb the killing energy being sent out by the corner. The plant will suffer from this continuous attack of killing energy and so it is necessary to change the plant every two to three months.

If you are using a wind chime to slow down the energy of a long corridor, make sure you use a wind chime that has five rods. It is the five-rod wind chime which has the counter energy to slow down killing chi. A wind chime with six, eight or nine rods is used for energizing, creating good chi. These will be dealt with later.

Lights are also very effective for dampening bad energy. A well-lit house or apartment generally has better feng shui than one that looks dim and has diffused lighting throughout. Residents in such homes often suffer all kinds of ailments unless during the daylight hours a great deal of sunlight somehow makes it into the home.

Energizing for acclaim with lights

A much better use of lights is to create the kind of lighting in the home which functions as a powerful magnet for drawing in acclaim and fame luck. This does not necessarily mean that you have to keep the south side of your home fully lit with spotlights all the time. Indeed, I am not in favour of spotlights since this creates a situation of excessive yang energy. Spotlights are blinding and it is like looking directly at the sun which then burns you. Temper the use of lights with the need for a good balance of yin and yang energy.

I have already spoken about my great preference for crystal chandeliers: the light reflected off the facets of cut crystal creates exactly the kind of energy required. For those who cannot afford these expensive trimmings, simply make sure that the whole south corner is well lit by a well placed light at the ceiling. Let the light seem to shine upwards to engender a sense of upward moving energy. Do make sure that the ceiling is white as this also creates also the feeling of yang. White, yellow and red are the ultimate yang colours.

If you have a garden, it is also a good idea to keep the south side of the garden well lit. In my house the south side of my garden is kept energized all through the night and day because I have placed my dogs there. The barking of the dogs represent life activity and excellent yang energy. The light on my south side is also always kept on during the nights. I need all this yang energy to bring me success in my work as a writer.

The precious yang energy of fire

The other manifestation of yang energy that is ideal for the south is the presence of fire. Thus fireplaces and their locations within households in temperate countries, where the winter season brings enormous yin cold energy, become extremely important.

A fireplace located on the south wall of the living room is the most ideal and auspicious. Apart from generating good fire element energy during the yin winter months, the fireplace also acts as an energizer for attracting the luck of recognition. They are also auspicious when placed along the southwest or northeast wall and less auspicious when placed along the north wall of a room.

If you do not have a fireplace, create a place in the south wall where you can have lighted candles. I have a small altar on the south side of my living room where I make light offerings each day. That is when I light my candles and although these represent my offerings to the holy object placed in that corner of the room, the candles also serve to create good yang energy that benefits my family. If you decide to use candles please make sure you remember that naked flames must always be handled with care, never leave a naked flame burning when there is no one around.

Energizing the phoenix

The south is also the place of the phoenix, one of the four celestial animals of the feng shui pantheon. The phoenix is the king of all winged creatures who have the ability to fly and soar to the skies. When the phoenix is symbolically placed in the front of the home, and in full view of the main front door, it is said to attract the luck of opportunities. In landscape school feng shui, the presence of the phoenix is signified by the presence of a small boulder in front of the door.

The phoenix is believed to possess so much energizing yang energy that it has the power to rise above the meanest of circumstances. From the heat of fire and ashes, the phoenix is said to rise and soar to the skies. This symbolism brings enormous power to its image when activated in the south. If you hang a picture of a crimson phoenix on the south wall of your study your work will be recognized, and you will benefit from outstanding fame luck. You can also use this method in your office or living room but never in the bedroom. A red phoenix in the bedroom will make your mind so active you will not be able to sleep.

Substitutes for the phoenix can also be used with equally good effect. If you happen to be born in the year of the rooster, you can place an image or picture or even a ceramic sculpture of this proud bird in the south of your living room.

Indeed, the rooster is described as a particularly excellent earth substitute for the phoenix, which is a creature of heaven. The rooster's body symbolizes many virtuous qualities. Thus the crown on his head is a mark of literary skill and suggests a passion for academia and learning. The spurs on his feet symbolize courage and bravery in the face of difficulties. His reliability is represented by the fact that he never fails to announce the start of every new day. So display a rooster in the south corner of your desk to symbolize these virtuous qualities. You will surely attract positive recognition of your own good qualities as a result of doing so.

Another winged creature that is regarded as being auspicious is the beautiful and stunning peacock. The feathers of this bird are used to symbolize attainments that are associated with being recognized. Thus peacock feathers are believed to attract honours being bestowed on the family patriarch. If you cannot find a picture of a peacock, you can use its feathers and work them into a flower arrangement for the south.

5 An abundance of success

'Inner feng shui
Enhances the harmony
Between inner
consciousness and
The physical outward
plane of your
personal space.
Purifying the mind
is as vital
as purifying the space.'

FENG SHUI is very much about success and achieving success. If you arrange your living space according to feng shui principles, you will be embraced by an aura of success that will also bring great abundance. Being surrounded by an air of achievement produces a strong aura of confidence that in turn creates a positive attitude. This brings yet more success. It is like stepping onto an expanding spiral of upward mobility. It engenders a happiness that can be very infectious and catching. Happiness often makes for yet more happiness. Therefore, if you want to attract prosperity and joy into your life you must endeavour to feel happy!

People who are achievement oriented rarely allow small inconveniences to irritate or annoy them. They see only the big picture and seldom breach the harmony of energies that surround them by breaking into anger. This mental attitude is a reflection of the unconscious inner feng shui they are practising to balance beautifully with the feng shui of their physical space. Inner feng shui requires a state of mental equilibrium that comes with a calm and relaxed disposition. Meditation helps to create this disposition, as does suitable visualizations that calm the inner spirit.

Success energies should be created internally as well as externally. You cannot enjoy optimum attainments unless your inner-self reflects a similar state of balance as your outer physical environment. The practice of feng shui to cultivate this state of balance in your outer space must always be in tandem with a real effort at creating inner equilibrium. One helps the other, so bring a relaxed and confident attitude to your efforts at attracting success chi into your personal space.

Creating inner equilibrium begins with an internalized clarification on what success means for you personally. You will always benefit from thinking things through before embarking on anything. The rearrangement of your space to attract success is no different. Establishing clear goals helps enormously in the actualizing process. Thinking your goals through will clarify your mind and make you see the different layers and dimensions of your success equations.

In the beginning it is not necessary to worry about how goals are to be achieved. It is sufficient to focus on the desired end results. Positive energies that are generated by your mind will always combine fruitfully with any of the positive energy flows of your environment. The marriage of the two collections of harmonious energies will help to actualize what you want.

Generating positive energy is like creating internalized feng shui. This involves mentally arranging pictures in your mind that place you in centre stage benefiting from the vibrations of your personalized space. It helps if you also make strong positive statements to yourself. You must believe in yourself and your abilities to actualize all your goals. Only then will your inner feng shui mesh positively with the feng shui of your physical space. Remember that the positive energies created by your mind are very powerful. But then so are its negative energies. Unless you have faith in, and believe in, yourself you will simply be sabotaging your own efforts, whatever they may be.

If you work through a programme of positive word affirmations that penetrate into your subconscious mind, you will be empowering your inner success energies even more. Remember that any positive statement is an affirmation and you can create a programme of success energies in any way that is comfortable to you.

You can condition yourself into thinking these positive affirmations each morning or at night just before you go to sleep. You can also work the affirmations into a daily routine. Whatever you do, the idea is to affirm your belief in yourself, that you can be a successful person, that you deserve to be a successful person.

Strengthened by these daily affirmations you will find feng shui practice and remedies a lot more fun because then you will be more relaxed. As a result, whatever you do from a feng shui viewpoint will surely be more accurate and more correct, thereby enhancing your chances of success. Furthermore, you will also be imbuing whatever you do with a healthy dose of positive energy and this will speed up the effect and potency of your feng shui practice. Done in this manner there is simply no way you can possibly fail!

Discarding negatives that block success

A vital part of the positive programming exercise involves discarding all the negative energies that stand in the way of you achieving success. There are two excellent techniques for clearing your mind of blocks that prevent positive winning energies from flowing.

The first involves a mental spring-clean. Over the years, all of us accumulate tons of mental excess baggage, which create blocks within our psyche. These blocks prevent us from attaining our objectives by constricting the flow of energy, not only within ourselves, but often also on the physical plane. These blocks work just like killing energy and they must be dissolved if we are to let the energies flow smoothly.

How do mental blockages build up and accumulate? Often they are caused by repressed emotions such as fear, guilt, anger and frustration arising from disappointments, the loss of a dear one, perceived injustices. And most of all from the constant negative programming that many of us were inundated with and subjected to since childhood.

Inside many of us is a lifetime of negative programming. We believe the world is not a safe place. We believe life is a struggle. We believe it is noble to suffer. We believe it is our lot to be poor, that having fun is wrong, that love is dangerous because we will get hurt. We believe that politics is dirty, that the root of all evil is money and that life is fated.

These are beliefs, nothing more. Certainly, they are not necessarily objective truths. They appear true only when we believe them to be true. Mental blockages such as these are usually deeply rooted and negative. They are emotional hindrances that subdue our inherent spirit and suppress our natural vitality, our intrinsic yang energy. They will work against all the good feng shui we put into place unless we get rid of them from our minds.

Surely it is not difficult to understand how such emotional blocks can damage a person's sense of self-esteem. To an extent, waves of uncertainty and feelings of unworthiness will weigh down any potential success from entering the front door. They act like barriers that prevent the house from accepting the success energies that want to enter. This is because often the fear of failure, of ridicule and of being hurt are so strong they become etched in stone and become real obstacles to success. They act like a big mountain in front of the main front door!

To get the flow of energy moving, it is necessary to clear these heavy blockages. It is necessary to change our negative beliefs by undertaking a mental spring-cleaning. To do this effectively, start by accepting your own personal limiting attitudes and beliefs. Identify the true nature of your fears. Usually, simply focusing on constrictive beliefs in this manner and accepting the feelings that surround it is often sufficient to make the negative attitude dissolve and disappear. This is the clearing process and it works like magic in freeing you from being severely hampered by invisible but powerful barriers.

Mental spring-cleaning is also wonderfully uplifting. It transforms your view of the world and of yourself. It brings all that you have ever wanted to be and to have enticingly within reach. Once you feel this attitude, the practice of feng shui becomes a breeze and you will enjoy putting those of its recommendations that you can use into place. You will also be able to discard recommendations that are simply not practical for your home and not feel worried about it.

In addition to mental spring-cleaning, it is also a good idea to clear all other barriers. This is because there is a whole lot of other emotional baggage that we all carry through life. I am referring especially to the holding of grudges, and the nurturing of thoughts that drain you of energy. Thoughts of getting even soaks up energy. It is truly exhausting maintaining negative feelings towards those whom we perceive have mistreated us, harmed us, done us an injury and bad-mouthed us.

Yes, you have every justification to feel aggrieved. Yours is a righteous ire. It feels right to be angry. But let me tell you that it really does feel better to forgive and release yourself. Forgiveness creates a powerful sense of liberation because it is like unleashing a dam of suppressed negative energies. Many people find the process miraculous in freeing them of their burdens of accumulated resentments and hostility. Some have described the experience as actual relief of heavy baggage off their backs.

This sort of mental clearing exercise often results in all physical overhanging barriers and obstacles magically disintegrating, in defiance of conventional logic. I remember I once had a tree growing in my neighbour's garden that sent a singular and harmful poison arrow towards my front door. I resented the tree very much and I felt the killing energy being sent my way. Since I have a personal aversion to using the Pa Kua mirror I decided the only thing to do was to place a wind chime above my door to dispel at least some of the harmful energy being sent my way. And then I let the tree go.

Mentally I said goodbye to the tree and refused to harbour any more negative feelings towards it. Believe it or not, within two months the tree that had caused me so much worry, shrivelled, turned brown and died!

You may well ask if it was the wind chime that did the job or my own mental attitude of letting go. I think it was a combination of both things – by letting go, the negative energy was deflected, and the wind chime physically returned any negative energy coming towards my door.

Defining meanings of success

Before looking at all the success methods of arranging physical space according to feng shui, there is one last thing left to do. This involves mentally clearing any negative energies being sent your way by other players in your scenario of success. It also simultaneously enhances any positive energies of outsiders who can assist you gain success.

Basically, this takes care of what we in feng shui refer to as the devil men and the heaven men in your life. Usually the success of individuals and corporate entities depends on the extent of sabotage or help that is created by devil men or sent by heaven men. Success often depends on the approval, consent or help of people who are for you or against you. Everyone has their fair share of admirers and enemies. It is advisable to undertake clearing exercises (see box, below) to diffuse the negative energies of devil men.

Defining your meaning of success is the next step in focusing the mind for success. I do not need to tell you that success means different things to different people and in using feng shui, it is helpful to know of the meanings for the ancients. When the ancient texts talk of great good fortune or prosperity, what exactly do they mean by these extravagant descriptions? Are there cultural differences in the way

Clearing exercise

To practise clearing exercises, send symbols of love and peace and good-will towards everyone you can think of who may have reason (or not) to dis-like you and therefore would harm you. Visualize a host of white doves, hearts and even kisses flowing towards your enemies from you. Soften your own attitude towards your enemies and then feel the whoosh of relief.

For more hardened and difficult enmities, you might want to perform this little ritual. Write down their names on a piece of paper and, if you like, describe the cause and nature of the enmity. Often the act of writing exact details will give you a fresh perspective to the situation. Then mentally let go by throwing the paper away, or if you want to make it stronger, imbue it with yang energy by burning it.

These acts of mentally clearing blockages involving third parties will help you clear the way to receiving help from the cosmos when you energize for success luck with feng shui. You have freed all the pathways to success.

the East and the West define success? I would say no, although the priorities of aspirations do differ. These differences do not pose a problem if we are clear about the kind of success that engenders in us a feeling of abundance.

The best way of clarifying your thoughts is to sit and write down all that you want from life in an organized way. It is unnecessary to be too complicated or profound. Keep your aspirations simple and straight-forward. But keep them clear and prioritize them. Categorize your success definitions under meaningful headings and rank them in importance to you. Thus, do you define success in terms of money, career, lifestyle, relationships, leisure time, family, personal growth, love, power, possessions, recognition, specific achievements, winning or having a great and healthy body?

These are only suggested ways of looking at success and the average person wants almost all of what I have written. It is only in the ranking in importance of all these things that you can get into a muddle, but by spending some time thinking through your order of priorities you can achieve greater success luck with feng shui.

Feng shui can be a very exact and precise practice and there are situations where you can be faced with choices such as what kind of success luck you wish to energize. It may be that you cannot have two types of success at any particular time and you have to choose. For instance, in the eight mansions school you have four good directions to choose from, each of which symbolizes a different type of success. You can tap only one direction when you sleep and so you will have to decide which direction best corresponds to what you want. It is the same when it comes to selecting which room you want as your office or as your bedroom since different locations spell different types of luck.

For example, if your Kua number is 1 and you want to energize for personal growth, you need to tap the direction of north as outlined on pages 63–4. But if you want to tap your sheng chi, or success and wealth direction, you need to make use of the southeast (see pages 88–90). For good health, the auspicious direction is east (see pages 97–8) and to create an abundance of love, the direction to enhance is south (see page 120).

In consciously planning out all that you want from life there is already inherent determination in the process. This adds vital success energies to the entire process. Now that you have clarified your thoughts here are some vital feng shui techniques to surround yourself with success energies. You can also go to the chapter that best addresses what you want to achieve.

Creating a winning main door

Probably the most important part of your home to attend to in terms of feng shui is your main door. This is the *kou*, or mouth, of your yang abode. It is where the entire good fortune chi that is meant for your home enters and accumulates.

The main door of a home is the door that you most frequently use to get into and out of your house or apartment. It is not a gate that stands outside, and nor is it any side doors. If there is a gate leading to your house this is also important and should be protected as well, but it is the main door that should engage most of your attention. If you live in an apartment, it is not the door that enters into the building where your apartment is situated. However, this general main door is also important in that if it is afflicted then everyone living in the entire apartment block will feel the negative results of such an affliction.

Try to observe as many of the guidelines listed opposite as possible. When you have assured yourself that your main door is not being afflicted in any way you can proceed to study the various ways of energizing the front door to bring you an abundance of success. But your door must not be afflicted. This is because everything you do to energize it simply will not work if it is being hit by bad energies.

Tapping your success direction is probably the best way of making your main door work for you. This method is based on the eight mansions formula which, in turn, is based on your Kua number. Refer to page 62 to determine your Kua number and then use the table on page 90 to determine the most auspicious direction for you in terms

General guidelines about main doors

◆ Main doors should be solid rather than be made of glass or see-through plastic.

◆ Doors that have two leaves are usually preferred to single leaf doors. It is fine if the two pieces that make up the door are of unequal size as long as it is the larger size piece that is opened the most frequently.

◆ Poison arrows in the outside environment should never directly hit main doors. Thus you should make very sure that your main door does not face a straight road coming directly at it. If the straight road is lower than the door it is not so harmful but, otherwise, hanging a yin Pa Kua is vital. Similarly, the triangular pointed shape of a neighbour's house should not hit the main door. Roads and roof lines often cause the most harm to main doors, so do watch out for them.

◆ Main doors should face open space. This is known as the Bright Hall effect and is most auspicious. Thus, houses whose main door opens to playing fields and empty land usually benefit enormously from this feature.

◆ Main doors should never face higher land. If the contours of the land slope downward so that it is lower behind the house than in front, the situation is most inauspicious. In such a situation, you should either change the door direction, or if this is not possible, hang a fairly sizeable mirror to reflect the mountain in front. In any case, this situation is not good and should be corrected as soon as possible.

◆ Any furniture placed outside should never be allowed to block your main door. You must always make sure that the way into your home never gets blocked since physical impediments easily translate into blockages in your life, preventing you from enjoying success in any of your endeavours.

◆ Any lane or path leading to your main door should be curved and preferably winding. A straight path that leads directly into your home sends slivers of killing energy. Such a path should also not narrow out or in. It is best when the width of the path stays constant. Placing lights on the pathway is auspicious.

◆ The main door of your home should not open into a toilet, staircase, straight line of other doors or a cramped space. The main door should also not face a wall with a mirror on it. This reflects away any good fortune that may be coming into your home.

◆ For the main door to be auspicious it should have good lighting both inside and outside. When the foyer area in the vicinity of the main door is well lit it attracts in chi and if the door is located in the south corner, or is facing the south corner, having this light becomes doubly auspicious.

◆ The main door should never be located directly under a toilet that is located on the floor above. This is a very inauspicious situation and residents living inside such a home will suffer from ill health. Success is difficult and there can be no abundance. One way of dealing with this problem is to shine a bright light upwards, but this should only be a temporary solution.

of success and wealth. This is described as your sheng chi direction and aligning your main door to directly face this direction will bring you an abundance of success luck. This can come either as improved income or in the form of advancement in your career.

Establishing your sheng chi direction

Your Kua number	Your success or sheng chi direction	Best designs of door	Best colour for door
1	southeast	rectangular	green, brown
2	northeast	square	earth, ochre
3	south	triangular	red, maroon
4	north	wavy	black, blue
5	northeast for men, southwest for women	square	earth, ochre
6	west	round	white
7	northwest	round	white
8	southwest	square	earth, ochre
9	east	rectangular	green, brown

Based on the table above you can use the last two columns to give you ideas on how else to energize the door to make it lucky for you. These suggestions on design motifs and colours are based on the door direction. They use the theory of the five elements to offer additional enhancement to your door. You can use these suggestions as long as the door is facing the direction indicated.

Shaping a lucky bedroom

These directions can also be used to help you to orientate your sleeping direction. If you can sleep with your head pointed to your sheng chi direction, you will benefit from the most personally excellent energies that will come your way each night as you sleep. Select a bedroom that allows you to orientate your head in this most auspicious direction. This may not always be possible since there are other feng shui guidelines that you must follow. For example, if you are sleeping in a bed that is afflicted by the furniture, corners and beams inside your bedroom then no matter if your sleeping direction is auspicious it will still be negatively affected by the bad surroundings. As such, it is useful to observe the general guidelines of bedroom feng shui outlined opposite and then consider the other, more stringent, guidelines for an auspicious bedroom summarized here.

Guidelines for good bedroom feng shui

◆ The ideal harmonious bed is one with a single mattress, which can be of a double bed dimension, that is oriented correctly to an auspicious direction. Poison arrows inside the bedroom should not hit it directly, and it needs to be luxurious and comfortable. The headboard can be decorated with auspicious embroidery, as can the pillowcases and bed sheets.

◆ To start with, regular shaped rooms are always better and superior to irregular shaped rooms: the best shapes are rectangular or square. L-shaped bedrooms should be corrected by positioning a screen to create two separate spaces.

◆ The bed should not be placed between two doors, or directly pointed at the entrance door. When the bed is between two doors, the energy of the doors cuts severely into the chi of the bed and the consequences on the sleeping person's health will be negative. When the feet point towards the door, this is said to be the death position, a curtailment of life.

◆ Make sure there are no sharp edges directly hitting at the sleeping position. The edge can come from the corner of two walls, or the edge of cupboards. They can be protruding corners or they can be stand-alone square pillars. All these situations lead to a negative effect on the health of the sleeping resident since killing chi is being sent to the sleeping form. The impact on the health of that person is therefore negative and even though the head may well be pointing in an auspicious direction, this good feature is completely obliterated by killing energy. Children are especially affected by this situation.

◆ The bed should not be located directly under an exposed overhead beam, a ceiling fan or an exposed apex of roof lines. When you are sleeping under something hostile, sharp or heavy, it presses down on your health thereby causing you to have very low resistance to illness and disease. At the best, you will merely be plagued by migraines and headaches. At its worse, the bad fortune could come in the form of severe illness. Also, beams that separate a couple will cause a rift to develop. It is better to cover them with a false plaster ceiling and

pretty cornices, or move the bed from under them. Sloping ceilings are also less than ideal but if you have no choice, sleep with the head under the highest part of the ceiling.

◆ You should not be able to see the toilet from the bed. Nor should the bed be placed directly under a toilet on the floor above. The effect of the toilet on the sleeping person's health will be very severe. Ailments include constant susceptibility to coughs, colds and headaches. Toilets are also said to cause stomach problems and other illnesses associated with the digestive systems.

◆ The bed should not be placed floating in the centre of the room. This suggests instability and is most inauspicious. In this connection, the bed should be firmly fixed and not seem to be falling apart.

◆ The bed should not be placed directly under a window since this also suggests a lack of stability. If you sleep this way, the chances are that you will travel a great deal and spend little time in your bed.

◆ Nor should the bed be placed against a wall that has a window directly above it. This causes the person to have sleepless nights and succumb to illnesses associated with fevers and body aches. If you have no choice, however, do try to sleep with curtains pulled close and make certain they are at least made of a fairly heavy chintz.

◆ The best place for the bed is diagonal to the entrance door and with a solid wall behind since this gives stability to the sleeping occupant. If the bed can then be made to point to the best sheng chi direction of the occupant it will be the most auspicious.

◆ If, for some reason, it is not possible to orientate the bed so the head is pointed to the sheng chi direction, then it is vital to choose one of the other directions in the same group of directions. If you an east group person (see page 63), the auspicious directions are east, southeast, north and south. If you are a west group person, the auspicious directions are west, southwest, northeast and northwest.

Mirrors

Strenuously avoid having the bed reflected in a mirror. The presence of exposed mirrors in the bedroom is often the cause of married couples splitting because of the entrée of a third party into the marriage. It causes infidelity and although it does not directly cause problems for the prosperity of the household, mirrors do cause a great deal of unhappiness. Mirrors facing each other are even worse since basically this causes severe disturbance to the mind. The infinite number of reflections caused by two mirrors directly facing each other is a serious and most inauspicious feature. Please either place a curtain to cover these mirrors or do away with them altogether. If you need to have a dressing table place it so that the mirrors do not reflect the bed. Alternatively, use the bathroom mirror or have a separate dressing area. I have seen mirrors cause so much havoc in marriages that I always talk about this feature. See also page 125.

Water features

You should also try not to have a water feature in the bedroom as it is said to have the same negative effect as reflecting mirrors. If you place an aquarium in the bedroom and it is directly behind your bed I can say with certainty that you will lose money or be robbed. Try also to avoid having water motifs in your paintings and furniture in the bedroom, although this is not as serious as having a painting of a lake, a waterfall or a river. Some feng shui masters have told me that having such a painting hanging above the bed is inauspicious since this seems to bring big water into the bedroom. This does not mean you cannot have a glass of water, a small refrigerator or a jug inside the bedroom. For feng shui purposes, these are not considered to be water features.

I have a very dear friend who once hung a beautiful painting of Venice above her bed. Soon after that, her husband developed severe back problems and had to be hospitalized. Unaware of this, I happened to be visiting them last summer when I saw this beautiful painting above her bed. I warned my friend about it and said that it could well cause either she or her husband or both to become hospitalized. It was then that she told me about her husband's excruciating back problems

. . . needless to say she removed the painting and re-hung it in the living room. I am happy to say that his back is now cured.

Live plants

Another object that could cause problems in the bedroom are live plants. Contrary to popular expectation, the placement of flowers and plants in the bedroom is not an auspicious feature. Plants represent the yang energy of growth and in other parts of the house they are quite excellent. In the bedroom, however, they do cause problems to sleeping occupants as they tend to sap the energy of the residents during the night. Plants are especially harmful where there is also a lack of sunlight. So instead of using plants to counteract shar chi from corners in bedrooms, hang a bamboo tied with red thread just above the edge, or place a screen to cover the corner from where you sleep.

Other objects to avoid in the bedroom are sharp objects, guns and paintings of animals. These hostile creatures will cause more harm than good and will seriously impair the feng shui of your bedroom.

Designing an auspicious office

The sheng chi direction should also be incorporated into your office design. To attract an abundance of success luck, always sit facing your sheng chi direction. Simply tapping this auspicious direction at work will reap you an abundance of huge benefits. However, in so doing it is vital that you also observe the other general guidelines that apply to office feng shui. Thus do try to incorporate the guidelines given overleaf into your office design.

If after observing the general guidelines overleaf you can also sit facing your sheng chi direction you will have successfully tapped your success direction at work. This is the most excellent energizer for career success and to ensure you do not forget to use a compass and mark out with an arrow on your desk the exact path of your sheng chi direction.

Use feng shui dimensions to create your good fortune desk. The dimensions for an executive desk are 152 x 89 cm (60 x 35 in). The

Guidelines for good office feng shui

- Let your office have a regular rather than an irregular shape. If the shape is irregular try to use plants and mirrors to regularize it.
- Do not locate your office at the end of a long corridor. This causes you to suffer from bad feng shui and you will find it difficult to have success.
- Do not place the office directly next to the toilet and, especially, you should not be sharing a wall with a toilet. In the same way, do not sit directly under a toilet on the floor above.
- Make sure that the foyer in your office is not too cramped since this reduces the flow of good fortune chi entering your office.
- Never sit with your back to the door. This will cause you to be stabbed in the back. In fact, you should never place your chair or desk in a way that you cannot see people entering the room. In feng shui this is described as a potentially dangerous situation. However,

also don't sit with the door directly in front of you.
- Never sit with your back to the window either. You must always have something solid behind you, and if you can have a wall on which you can hang the picture of a mountain it will assure you of much needed support. Remember that at work or in business, support is a vital ingredient of success, whether it is from your superiors or from your customers and your financiers. In fact, how successful you are often depends on the extent of support you can garner.
- Never sit directly under an exposed overhead beam. It will seriously impair your judgements and the decisions you make. In the same way, do not sit directly in the line of fire from the killing energy being sent your way by sharp edges of protruding corners. Place a plant to dissolve such negative energies.

height of the desk should be 84 cm (33 in). If you like, you can also energize the table top with good feng shui. This is particularly effective if you apply the five element theory so that you have auspicious symbols like dragons and tortoises carved as decorative items on the sides and drawers of your table.

The executive chair you sit on should have a high back to symbolize back support. Chairs that do not completely cover your back represent poor feng shui. Your chair should also have armrests. If there are no armrests, this means the celestial animals – the dragon and tiger – are missing and you will lack protection in your work. Use a height of 109 cm (43 in) for the back of your chair. This brings prosperity luck.

Make sure that your office is always well lit. When offices are not properly lit the feng shui suffers because yang energy is weakened. Also make sure that if the afternoon sun comes in that it does not get too hot. Too much strong energy makes for excessive yang energy and this too is inauspicious. Feng shui is very much about balancing the energies of yin and yang.

Another important feng shui item, which should be placed in the office, is a live plant that is growing healthy and lush. The presence of a plant represents growth energy because the energy movement of the wood element is upwards. This is symbolically excellent for the office. The plant should be placed either in the east or southeast corner of the office.

Tapping personal success locations

In addition to tapping the auspicious sheng chi direction, it is also important to tap the sheng chi location. In practising feng shui it is necessary to differentiate between the direction and the location of a space. Both are equally important and when it is not possible to tap the direction you should try to tap the location that is auspicious and vice versa.

Once you know the direction that will bring you success, locate the corner of your house that corresponds to that direction. Refer to the Lo Shu grid that was superimposed on your home or apartment. This will indicate the sheng chi location of your home. If you are able to place either your bedroom or your study in this corner you will be energizing the luck of location. And then, depending on which element is represented by the location, you can energize it by placing objects that enhance or produce that element.

For example, if your sheng chi is the east, the element will be wood. If your study or office is located here you can enhance the energies by introducing a water feature as water enhances wood. If your bedroom is located in the east, however, placing a water feature would be inappropriate since bedrooms should never be energized with water.

When deciding on what symbols to use to enhance any corner, a safe rule of thumb is to identify the element represented by the corner (see page 140) and then introduce something that belongs to an element that produces that element. You cannot go wrong when you enhance your space using five element theory.

6 An abundance of good health

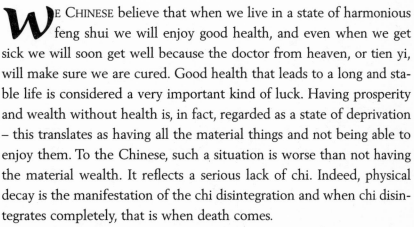

Focus on nourishing the chi.
The outer chi makes your environment
*   healthy.*
The inner chi makes you healthy.
Both are important.'

WE CHINESE believe that when we live in a state of harmonious feng shui we will enjoy good health, and even when we get sick we will soon get well because the doctor from heaven, or tien yi, will make sure we are cured. Good health that leads to a long and stable life is considered a very important kind of luck. Having prosperity and wealth without health is, in fact, regarded as a state of deprivation – this translates as having all the material things and not being able to enjoy them. To the Chinese, such a situation is worse than not having the material wealth. It reflects a serious lack of chi. Indeed, physical decay is the manifestation of the chi disintegration and when chi disintegrates completely, that is when death comes.

All traditional Chinese practices – from acupuncture to physical exercises, herbal cures, massages and, of course, feng shui – focus on nourishing the chi, both externally in the surrounding environment as well as internally through meditation and breathing exercises. This concept of chi is based on the belief that all things in the Universe, tangible and intangible, alive and inanimate, possess the magical consciousness of chi. Thus, every room in the home and every cell in the human body has its own intrinsic energy which the Chinese call chi.

Thus chi kung, for example, teaches that nourishing the chi within through internalized exercises effectively supplements external feng shui. This nourishing of chi is what leads to good health and long life, which features prominently in the feng shui list of human kind's aspirations. An abundance of good health is as valuable as an abundance of great wealth, and health bringing chi is as easy to harness as the kind of chi that brings wealth.

For example, the eight mansions method of formula feng shui addresses health luck as well as wealth lucks and there is a special auspicious direction which is called tien yi direction. This is the direction which, when properly harnessed into the orientations of beds, doors and desk placements, will specifically ensure good health and long life. This is the direction that is usually recommended as being excellent for the older generation of an extended family.

As with the sheng chi direction (see pages 88–90), the tien yi direction is based on a person's Kua number (see page 62). The table right offers the most auspicious health direction according the Kua numbers. Check this table to identify the personal auspicious health direction of every member of your family, and then try to tap these directions in at least one of three ways. These ways are:

- sleeping in a tien yi location,
- sleeping with the head pointed in a tien yi direction or
- staying in a bedroom whose door faces out in a tien yi direction.

It is not necessary to have all three features. One is usually sufficient.

Sleeping in a tien yi location requires the relevant direction to be identified using the Lo Shu square. Once the house or apartment has been divided into nine equal grids, and the direction of each grid has been identified, it becomes easy to locate the most auspicious place in the apartment for a sickly or elderly person. Simply match the tien yi direction taken from the table and identify the relevant location. Then try to have a bedroom there and allocate this bedroom to the sick person. This will greatly facilitate recovery. In addition to the location, the sick person should also try to sleep with the head pointing in the tien yi direction. The heavenly energies that cure illness come from the tien yi direction. Make certain, however, that in doing this you also observe the guidelines for good bedroom feng shui as described on pages 90–93.

Establishing your tien yi direction

Your Kua number	Your health or tien yi direction
1	east
2	west
3	north
4	south
5	west for men, southwest for women
6	northeast
7	southwest
8	northwest
9	southeast

Balancing yin and yang

As well as positioning the bed to capture the auspicious health direction based on eight mansions theory, yin and yang therapy can be applied to the bedroom to bring about good health energies.

To start with, the bedroom is a place of rest where calming and quiet, understated yin colours should be reflected in curtains, drapes and carpets. Yin ambience should rightly prevail, yet if there is an excess of yin, susceptibility to sickness is greatly magnified. Healthy bedrooms should always have a clearly visible yang presence and this is best represented by the presence of good and proper lighting. Lights are very yang, so it is necessary to guard against excessively bright spotlights. Flashy lights do a great deal more harm than good. Instead, go for small yet intensive red lights that are used in small doses. The red colour adds a note of vibrancy and it is very effectively yang, yet never so intense as to cause a problem.

Yang energy can also be introduced in the form of music, especially calming baroque music, and through turning on the radio. This kind of yang energy is not too harsh, nor too severe, yet it is uplifting and very good for nourishing chi. Play New Age music – the sounds of whales and dolphins, of jungle creatures in the morning sunrise, of flutes and tinkling bells – all of which make for a gentle inflow of yang energy that creates wonderful and healthy vibrations. These are especially soothing for invalids and convalescing patients because they create gentle yang energy that is good for the health yet not so strong as to cause problems for rest. This kind of yang energy supplements the yin energies of bedrooms in a very sustaining sort of way.

Yang energy should not be present in the form of live plants and flowers (see page 93). At the same time, yin energy should not be energized with the physical presence of a water feature (see page 92). If the bedroom is in the north, therefore, it is a good idea not to have a water feature even though I advise a water feature in the north! Instead, you would be better off energizing the water feature either in the living room, the family room or the garden.

The good health bedroom

I am often asked about bed headboards and canopies. Is there any feng shui significance to these bed accessories? The answer, of course, is yes. In the old days, wealthy families had elaborately decorated beds that were constructed to create a feeling of refuge. Antique Chinese bridal beds, for instance, will show you that they resemble box-like structures that have only one opening, and this too is often covered with a lace or brocade curtain.

The sleeping place is thus likened to a place of refuge, a sanctuary of some kind. Some beds even had windows along the sides so that those sleeping could look out of their beds, while still in bed! The curtains covering the bed would often be decorated with elaborate embroidery that had all the symbols of good fortune.

Young and newly married couples would have the hundred children screen embroidered on the bed to signify fruitful unions that would result in many sons. Older members of the family and especially the patriarch (*lo yeh*) would sleep on a bed that was surrounded by longevity and good health symbols.

In modern bedrooms, therefore, canopies that suggest a feeling of safety and refuge are welcomed. However, I prefer a full canopy to a half canopy since this latter design tends to suggest an overhang rather than a refuge. A four-poster bed is excellent, but a princess type fairy tale looking bed is not auspicious.

Headboards should be round and humped, resembling a tortoise. This would be the safest and most auspicious type of headboard as it gives protection against bad vibes and illness while you sleep. The shapes to avoid are the triangular, rectangular and wavy types of head-boards since they are not suitable for the bedroom. Triangular shaped headboards are suggestive of the fire element causing the bed to become excessively yang. Wavy headboards suggest the water element and this too is unsuitable for the bedroom. Rectangular headboards signify the wood element. This suggests growth, and is a suitable choice even though I advise against the physical presence of plants.

Creating a healthy bedroom implies that anything that might be causing the bedroom to be hit by excessively yin energies or by killing chi has either been removed or neutralized. In this connection, perhaps the most difficult feng shui affliction to correct is when the toilet is placed in a harmful orientation to the bed or to the entrance into the room. Toilets directly above the bed are also extremely harmful, as are toilets that are placed against the wall, which has a bed on the other side.

Suppressing yin energy in toilets

Attached toilets and bathrooms should always have their doors kept closed. This in itself, however, is insufficient as an antidote to the yin energies they emit. The surest way of pressing down the bad luck of toilets is to hang a five-rod wind chime inside the toilet, and if this is still insufficient, to paint the door into the toilet red. If it bothers you to have this a bright red, white is an excellent second choice. This creates sufficient yang energy to counter the bad chi. All shades of blue are considered inauspicious for toilets. Having either red/maroon carpet or hanging red curtains in the toilet can also create corrective yang energy. This is not an ideal situation but it will help to diffuse the corrupt energy of the toilet, and prevent it from accumulating or stagnating.

Another way to bring yang energy to the room is to place a bright light in the toilet. A single red light would be very effective since this creates the presence of the fire element, which burns the afflicted metal element made negative by the presence of the toilet. Do not place flowers or plants in the toilet. These cause more harm than good.

Displaying the symbols of longevity

Longevity features so strongly in the Chinese list of life aspirations that there are probably more symbols of longevity than any other abstract, and only symbols of prosperity and wealth come anywhere close. Longevity is a very important luck to create. Secondly, to the Chinese, a God always symbolizes every aspiration that is important to them. The Chinese pantheon of deities is therefore a long list of Gods that personify these collective aspirations. And so we have Gods of wealth, health and prosperity.

Perhaps the most popular of the deities is the God of longevity, or Sau. The God of longevity is a friendly old man with a large and broad forehead. He walks with the aid of a walking staff that is carved with the symbol of the dragon. He holds on to this staff with his left hand and in his right hand he holds another symbol of longevity, the peach. Sau is often drawn onto paintings or ceramic ware, or he is fashioned into a statue for decorative purpose. He is usually drawn with a deer and a pine tree in the background. These are other symbols of longevity. All these symbols are extremely popular with the Chinese who believe that displaying them in the house will create vibrant good health energies thereby causing residents to be free from diseases and illnesses that are fatal.

The God of longevity can be displayed on his own or as one of the three Star Gods collectively referred to as Fuk Luk Sau. These Star Gods are not worshipped by devotees. They are seen as symbols of aspirations and are not real deities. They can be placed in the dining room or located on a mantelpiece facing the main door. You can purchase them in any medium – as ceramics, ivory, wood or steel moulded statues or carvings.

Probably the most popular symbol of longevity and good health is the wonderful bamboo plant. If you have a garden it is a good idea to create a small bamboo grove in the east side. If you live in an apartment, look for a beautiful painting of the bamboo and place it in the east side of the living room.

Because the bamboo is regarded as a very auspicious plant, its stem can also be used as a very effective feng shui tool. When pairs of bamboo stems are tied with red string and hung on beams and corners they successfully ward off killing energy that create problems for residents. There are many different varieties of bamboo; those that have hollow stems are the most auspicious.

Another symbol of longevity that is very popular is the peach fruit. Eat plenty of peaches for good health. Even better, try to have a decorative peach tree in your living room – one made of jade would be nice! This is easy to buy from a Chinese supermarket. The peach features prominently in many old Chinese stories, and legend has it that it is the peach tree that grows in the garden of the Queen of the West that bears the fruit of immortality. Indeed, the famous Eight Immortals of Taoist folklore are said to have stolen into this garden and eaten the peach there to gain their immortal status.

Anything that symbolizes the peach would make a great birthday gift to an old patriarch or matriarch. When looking for works of art that depict the peach, look for those that have either five or nine peaches. The number five has the power to overcome misfortunes, while the number nine signifies the fullness of heaven and earth.

My favourite symbol of longevity is the beautiful crane. The cranes of longevity have a red forehead and they are usually drawn either in flight or standing in the water with one leg tucked under. Cranes are also drawn with the pine tree, which is yet another symbol of longevity. I have a sculpted model of a crane in the east corner of my garden, but they can be placed anywhere to signify good health and long life. In addition, I also have many ceramic containers that are drawn with these longevity cranes. But that is more because of my love for these beautiful birds than anything else. Nevertheless, every member of my family living in my home enjoys great good health!

Yet another great favourite of mine, and one that probably reflects my Chinese roots, is the tortoise. This is a creature that brings only good fortune to any household that has it. The tortoise (or turtle) is another symbol of longevity and having it in the home, either as a real live pet or as a fake decorative item or painting simply does wonders for the luck of the home. In addition to bringing great good fortune, however, the tortoise is also a symbol of support and protection. It signifies the celestial support of the north.

It is because of this that my favourite tip for everyone is to have a small tortoise pond in the north corner of your house, and preferably your garden. It does not matter if the north corner is in the back or the front of the house, or on the left or right of the main door. Keep the tortoises in a small ceramic container half-filled with water, feed them with fish food and watch them grow.

Avoiding illness-causing flying stars

If you want to specifically use feng shui to take care of your health, it is a good idea to learn about flying star feng shui. In Chinese, this formula is called fey sin feng shui and it is an advanced compass school formula that is based on the Lo Shu square.

Flying star feng shui is very popular in Hong Kong. It addresses the time dimension of feng shui and provides detailed indications of areas of the home that could be afflicted by the illness stars during certain months of certain years. When used in conjunction with the Chinese calendar, it reveals the placement of illness stars so that anyone staying in these specifically afflicted corners will succumb to severe illness (often fatal) during the week or month when the stars themselves become vulnerable.

This formula is difficult for the amateur. Understanding the calculations and their interpretations requires a thorough understanding of feng shui fundamentals. For the beginner reading this book, however, I have calculated the dangerous corners that will be afflicted by flying illness stars over the next few years. You can refer to the table opposite and then check whether your bedroom happens to be located in the afflicted areas in each of the coming years. If it is, then during that year it is advisable to move to another room so that you do not succumb to any severe illness. This same analysis can be applied by everyone. Keep bedrooms that are located in the afflicted area empty through the period when it is being hurt by the afflicted illness star.

More severe in its effects than having the bedroom located in an afflicted area is when the main door to your home is located in the corner that is being hit by the illness stars. This situation is slightly more difficult to handle since an afflicted main door affects the whole family and, indeed, all the people living there. During the period when the door is suffering from the flying stars, if it is at all possible it is a good idea to stop using that door altogether and instead use another door into the home. If this is not possible, then try to be on holiday as much as possible so as not to get hit by the illness stars during the year (period) when the house is afflicted.

Placement of illness stars

Year	Afflicted corner	Very afflicted corner
1999	northwest	south
2000	west	north
2001	northeast	southwest
2002	south	east
2003	north	southeast
2004	southwest	centre
2005	east	northwest
2006	southeast	west

We are now in the period of 7, which started in 1984 and will end in the year 2003. The next 20-year period will be the period of 8 and that period runs to the year 2023. During this period of 7, the number 7 is a lucky number. The number 8 is also lucky and it indicates future prosperity. From 2004 onwards, during the period of 8, the number becomes even more lucky.

Mantra purification

Bedrooms should be symbolically energized with fresh energies on a regular basis to ensure that residents do not succumb to illnesses that are caused by stale and stagnant energies. The best way to do this is simply to air the room once a week.

Open at least two sets of windows in the house, one set of which should be inside the bedroom. Then, keeping the bedroom door open allow the breezes from outside to blow into the room, mingle with the energy inside and flow out again. This simple action will act like replacement therapy and freshen the chi in your bedrooms enormously.

This is also an excellent way of clearing the room of old energies that may have been left behind by a previous sick tenant. If you feel that you want the cleansing process to be stronger, you can use incense to purify the energies further. Those of you who wish to do so can chant either of the purification mantras given overleaf.

Whether the use of mantras is a part of feng shui is a debatable point but as far as I am concerned, the Chinese have always combined house purification with feng shui. In the old days, monks usually performed the rituals of purification. Lay people seldom had the capability to

Two purification mantras

1 Om Ah Hung So Ha

This is a purification mantra that is chanted by all Buddhists when they place offerings to the Buddha on an altar or shrine, or before they eat their meal and dedicate offerings to the Buddha. It is a powerful mantra that instantly purifies, and you can visualize all the objects in your rooms being purified as you move in and out of them with the incense. Simply repeat the mantra under your breath 108 times. Use a Buddhist rosary, called a mala, to count.

2 Om Mani Peh Me Hone

This is probably the most well-known of the Tibetan Buddhist mantras. It is the mantra that directly addresses the Compassionate Buddha who is known as Chenrezig to the Tibetans, Avolekiteshvara to the Hindus, the Goddess of Mercy Kuan Yin to the Chinese, and Canon to the Japanese.

It is a very, very powerful mantra and it is said that anyone who chants this mantra a million times (which may take one year to complete) will be endowed with a special gift like clairvoyance. Many Buddhists chant this mantra simply to invoke precious blessings from the Compassionate Buddha.

This mantra is extensively purifying. Chant it 108 times to cleanse the chi of your home. As you chant, move slowly around the walls of your home and visualize the sounds of your chanting causing the energies to become crystal clear with purity.

undertake mantra chanting. Nor did they have the expertise to ring the bells and clash the cymbals. In modern day house purification, many of the rituals have been simplified, which is something I have done in this book.

These rituals are founded on traditional practice but I have discovered that as long as my practice is based on fundamental concepts related to correct motivation and visualizations, the energies of the home always benefit from the incorporation of mantras into the purifying and cleansing rituals. For those of you who are not Buddhists, I humbly suggest that you use a similar prayer from your own religion to enhance your purifying exercises. I have discovered the cleansing operation works with any prayer or mantra that is chanted with a good heart and the correct motivation.

I love chanting these mantras all over my home to bless the energies that surround me. In this practical application of my feng shui knowledge I have combined my spiritual leanings with my feng shui methods. At first I did it because I did not see the harm in combining the method of my feng shui expertise with the wisdom of my spiritual beliefs. Later, as I observed my surroundings and the effect of this blending of wisdom and method, I found myself becoming healthier, more energetic, happier and also more successful. It seemed so complementary and so right.

It is because of this that I have included the simple mantras and rituals into this book, to share something I regard to be rather beautiful with my readers. This comes from my belief that it is not only wonderful but also potent to combine the method energies of feng shui with the wisdom energies of one's religious and spiritual practices. Hence, by linking the chanting of mantras with feng shui, the clearing of the physical space can be a very uplifting and effective exercise. It is definitely an excellent way of creating a healthy bedroom that brings a spring into your every movement. Make it a habit to cleanse and purify the energies of your bedrooms regularly. Indeed, make it a habit to purify your whole house on a regular basis. If it does not offend your own spiritual sensitivities I suggest that you might like to try purifying your personal space with the mantras and rituals given here.

Transcendental feng shui cure

In addition to physical feng shui, it is also possible to practise a special kind of transcendental feng shui which is particularly effective for creating curative energies that effectively supplement medical care for those who are suffering from serious diseases or illnesses. The method utilizes special visualization techniques and mantra chanting.

Transcendental feng shui uses two main visualizations of the mind: for physical enhancements of the surroundings and for the specific illness or disease being attended to. Often, when these visualizations are also accompanied with strong mantra chanting, the effect is almost miraculous. Not only do people get well they also get well so fast that it can be rather overwhelming.

So far, this chapter has directly addressed what needs to be done to create a healthy physical environment using feng shui guidelines and compass formulas. To empower these physical changes it is an excellent idea to also visualize your desired end result as you make changes to your physical surroundings.

You can do your visualizations at any time of the day or night, but the early mornings are the best time, just before dawn. Sit in a quiet room facing your tien yi direction to bring healing energies your way. Close your eyes, compose yourself, take a deep breath and relax before you begin.

Think, 'I am using this transcendental feng shui cure to supplement the physical feng shui changes I have already made.' Think of whatever is ailing you as blockages in the flow of your chi through your physical body. Those suffering from incurable diseases like AIDS, Cancer and other life-threatening diseases can visualize these ailments as severe blockages in their system.

Picture them as obstacles that must be removed. If you read up on the medical descriptions of what ails you, you will be able to be more vivid in your visualizations. Generate very strong energy to combat the illness that is causing your body to weaken and wither. Think very strongly but keep breathing to stay collected and in balance. Picture your mind strongly pushing the obstacle out of your system. In other words fight back. Mentally fight the illness.

Use the mind to create mental feng shui pictures that show your own intrinsic energy annihilating the bad energy that is causing you to get sick. Visualize blockages being dissolved inside you. Breathe deeply the fresh air and visualize this additional new energy entering your body and pushing through the blockages in your system . . . the stronger the visualization, the more powerful will be the effect and the faster it will work. Then picture all the bad energy transforming into black ink and flowing out of your body and going deep into the earth.

Practise this transcendental cure regularly until forming pictures in your mind becomes second nature and habitual. But do not look on this method as an alternative to proper medical care. It should be regarded as an additional way of being cured which complements whatever medical care you may be getting.

And now allow me to share a very powerful healing mantra with you. I have received permission from my very kind lama who transmitted it to me, to pass it on through this book to help those who may be very ill and are looking for an alternative healing system that might help. This mantra is that of the Medicine Buddha. Visualize the

Medicine Buddha above your head. This Buddha has a dark blue body and He is simply so beautiful. If you can, do go out and actively look for a picture to enable you to be more vivid in your visualizations. Chant the Medicine Buddha mantra seven times each morning and seven times each night. Chant it while doing the visualizations. If you chant with a sincere motivation, not only will you somehow get a picture of the Medicine Buddha, you will also feel yourself getting better. Here is the mantra:

Om Bhaykandze, Bhaykandze
Maha Bhaykandze Ratna Samu Gate Soha

Naturally, those of you who wish to do so can chant it more often. This would be even better. The mantra of the Medicine Buddha is believed to be extremely powerful and it is full of merit to chant the mantra regularly. It will be even better if you chant it for someone else – a loved one who is desperately ill, a grandfather, or simply a stranger you happen to come across. Buddhists believe that prayers that are dedicated to others are always extremely powerful.

7 An abundance of love

*'Tune in to the intensity of your own aura
  which is also your yang energy field.
This is the invisible light
Whose intensity reflects your energy
  levels.'*

IT IS a good idea to take a few moments each day to tune into yourself. It makes you feel grounded and balanced. Start by finding a quiet place somewhere. Then take several slow deep breaths. When you feel your body relaxing, allow a feeling of softness to come over you. Then tune into yourself. Focus on your being. Observe your own feelings, and experience a sense of loving. Let yourself savour the powerful welling up of affection and tenderness. Let this awareness spread laterally outwards towards those who live and work with you. Focus on this consciousness for a few minutes each day.

Connecting to the loving self within you becomes easier by the day, and it soon generates a loving disposition. This is an attitude that creates gentleness in the air and it is this attitude that makes you into a charming person surrounded by very positive energy, a positive energy that attracts. This very special brand of energy has an uncanny multiplier effect. If you want to attract love and loving into your life, you must make the effort to cultivate this kind of loving energy.

Tell yourself that from today, you will totally transform your attitude towards all the negatives, all the annoyances and annoying people in your life. You will not be too hard on yourself. You will not be overly critical, either of yourself or of others, when things go wrong or do not work out your way. You will go with the flow and you will start learning to love yourself unconditionally. By seeing yourself this way, you will begin to see others in this same light. You will develop a love of others in the same unconditional way.

This will open your eyes to the brighter side of people, situations and circumstances. When you are prepared to love yourself and others with no conditions attached, your energy field of goodwill starts to expand considerably. Look forward to receiving all the positive energies of the Universe. Start working with the magic of your own loving disposition. Smile a lot more and laugh at the humour of daily occurrences. Laughter is infectious and is terribly effective in generating strong positive energies. It also helps you to keep a long fuse so that things and people do not annoy or upset you easily.

Your aura or yang energy field

Tuning in to the loving side in you in this way strongly enhances your own aura or yang energy field. This is the invisible 'light' that surrounds every living creature. The intensity of this light reflects the concentration of the person's own inherent energy levels. The more yang you are as a person, the more powerful will be your aura.

The more powerful your aura is, the more you will be able to attract people into your life – people who love you and are drawn to you. Your aura reflects your own magnetism, your personal power. It is an incredibly uplifting feeling when you become aware of your own beautiful aura.

When you work at connecting with these inherent energies inside you, your chances of enhancing them will be magnified if your physical environment is in harmony with your own energies and is itself auspicious and balanced. This is where feng shui comes in. It enables you to create balance and harmony in the living space around you.

Auspicious space is created when you use any one of the many different feng shui methods available. The use of feng shui adds a powerful dimension to the creation of the magnetic and attractive personality: it can both activate and energize your own inherent chi.

Feng shui can bring about an environment that is saturated with an air of auspicious energies. Within such an environment it is easier to become a more confident, optimistic and up-beat person. This produces the attitude that will enable you to grasp the opportunities that feng shui will send your way. Indeed, when done correctly, feng shui will magnify your personal power so considerably and strongly it will enhance your special magnetism. Feng shui thus takes care of your external environment.

For maximum effect, I always recommend that feng shui corrections and enhancements should be undertaken in conjunction with what you are doing internally. Take your sense of humour, your laughter, and your feeling of confidence into the inner conscious levels of your mind. Go deep into your alpha planes – that part of yourself that can be accessed only in the semi-meditative state. Become aware of your sub-conscious mind deep within. Working with the sub-conscious mind in this way gives the added boost to achieving an abundance of love and loving relationships.

Visualize yourself surrounded by loud happy laughter, by stunning people who love you. Release the special vibrations that will add to the energies of your space. Remember that although feng shui addresses the placement and orientation of inanimate objects, ultimately it is the optimum balance of energies that creates good feng shui. In this, the strength of the human presence and their inherent energies is an important factor.

The human residents in any abode are the principal sources of yang energy. It is the living beings in any place that are the most yang, and who also need yang energy to grow, to develop, to stay alive and be healthy, and to be happy and contented. Positive minded and confident people are said to be very yang, and in turn generate a considerable amount of yang energy. This makes their space very auspicious, especially when it comes to attracting other icons of yang energy.

Have you noticed how happy, energetic and positive people always attract lots of people around them? And how negative, sour minded people always seem to repel people? Feng shui expresses this same kind of energy in the context of space. When we create active yang energy in the environment, the space becomes attractive and auspicious. Problems start when we have too much yin energy or when we introduce so much yang energy that we have overdone things. When there is too much yang, the yin energy ceases to exist, instantly killing yang energy as well. It is thus vital to get the balance correct. In this context, activate relationship feng shui to bring a load of loving into your life!

Improving social life with feng shui

Once the human personality is consciously aware of the yang energy field or aura, it is easy to understand that what is required from the start is the creation of a suitably yang atmosphere. There are many different ways of creating a more yang environment that in turn creates a busier social life without going overboard.

The correct practice of feng shui requires that energizing techniques and methods are never overdone to the extent that good feng

---

Energizing your main door

South
See main text, opposite.

North
If your door faces north or is in the north corner of your home, hang a six-rod wind chime in that corner. A wind chime will add strong yang energy to the sector and still balance well with the element of the north, which is water: metal creates water in the cycle of elements. The tinkling sounds of the wind chime will enhance the social life of residents, and if the southwest has also been properly energized, these relationships will then proceed smoothly and with few conflicts and misunderstandings.

East or southeast
If your door faces east or southeast, or is in the east or southeast corner of your home, place a single urn filled with water inside the door. The water should be placed on the left-hand side of the door as you look out. Change the water daily or three times a week, and don't cover it. The water will add wonderful vitality to the wood element of the corner. In addition, make sure that the foyer just inside the door is brightly lit. A lamp hanging from the ceiling will be better than a wall light since the whole area then gets lit up with yang energy. Doing this will also improve the overall feng shui luck of the house.

West or northwest
If your door faces west or northwest or is in the west or northwest sector of your home, place a painting of a mountain scene near the door. It would be great if the painting had twin peaks to symbolize the influence of the southwest whose number is two. It is even better if you can have a painting of mountain ranges that are rich with gold deposits. Do not have mountain peaks that look too sharp or triangular since this suggests the fire element. This element is unsuitable for doors that are located in corners signified by the metal element and the west and northwest are both metal element corners. If you cannot find a suitable painting, you can use decorative ceramic ware near the front door.

Northeast or southwest
If your door faces northeast or southwest, you will be dealing with earth energy and this is especially powerful for activating relationships luck. The southwest is the corner that is generally symbolic of love and marriage. The southwest is also the corner associated with mother earth as symbolized by the trigram kun. To stimulate either of these earth corners and create precious yang intensity, there is no better way than using bright sparkling lights. I am particularly fond of crystal chandeliers since these express the brightness of lasting friendships and relationships. Place a chandelier like this near the main door. It will not only improve your social life, the crystals and lights will attract the good fortune chi as well.

---

shui becomes bad feng shui. Or that an auspicious warm environment becomes void of existence. A state of non-existence is far worse than a totally silent environment that is excessively yin. This is a particularly important point to remember when it addresses feng shui methods that activate aspirations relating to social relationships, marriage, family and love.

Those of you who want to use feng shui methods to create a busier social life will benefit from a south-facing main door or a door that is located in the south section of the home or apartment. The south corner is that part of the home that is said to have a tremendous store of yang energy. At the same time, the south direction is also regarded as the direction from which a great accumulation of yang energy is derived. This is why a south-facing door or a south-located door are both well placed to be energized for a more active social life. If you wish to further strengthen the yang energy, a good way to do this is to paint your door red. You do not have to use a bright vermilion red. A darker maroon red will do just as well and is, in fact, better, as this is the yang of red balanced with a mixture of black which is yin. If your door does not face south, the box opposite describes the techniques you can use to energize for extra yang energy for the other seven directions.

Visualizing an ideal life partner

One of the great joys about being a feng shui writer is the way one can actually bring smiles onto faces, and the best response I get are from readers who have been brought together into a love match by my books. I never realized how many lonely hearts there were out there until I started receiving heartwarming thank-you letters from readers who had found each other after activating their love and marriage corners.

Many found the simple act of placing a pair of colourful mandarin ducks in the southwest side of their bedroom sufficient to open their eyes to romantic opportunities. Others discovered that the use of a bright and intense red light, again placed in the southwest corner, particularly potent in bringing love into their loves. There are many different ways of energizing for a wife or husband, but you have to be really sure and certain that you are ready for a commitment.

In the Chinese view of life and family, feng shui differentiates rather strictly between marriage and having a fling. In the Chinese tradition, love, marriage and family are all bound up to mean one and the same thing. Thus when you actively stimulate the elements of the southwest corner for marriage, you will be activating your family luck as well. Thus it is better not to energize marriage luck unless you are ready for marriage.

When you plant a long pole into the southwestern ground of your garden and install a light there – and if you keep this light turned on each night for at least three hours – you are activating marriage luck. The effect is that all sons and daughters of the family of marriageable age will soon find themselves being seriously wooed by suitors with honourable intentions. Marriage opportunities will be created. This particular technique is extremely powerful in bringing you a wife or a husband if you are single. It does not, however, guarantee a perfect spouse. It causes your marriage luck to ripen, but it does not ensure that the match will necessarily be a blissful or long lasting one. This part of the happiness equation is left to your mankind and heaven luck, ie to your own fate and karma.

This is why I always advise my single friends to visualize strongly the kind of mate they want. Have a strong and clear picture of the ideal life partner that you wish for. Unless you have thought it through, your own intrinsic energies will not help you to actualize someone who will make you truly happy. Usually when I speak about potential life partners most people either think about someone who is already in their lives; someone they are already dating but who is reluctant, as yet, to make a commitment, or they have no clue as to the kind of person they want.

Getting a reluctant boyfriend or girlfriend to commit to marriage is like trying to use feng shui to create a love potion. Unfortunately, feng shui does not work this way. You cannot use feng shui to make someone who is not interested in you become more so. You can, however, use feng shui to speed up the commitment process or to bring genuine marriage prospects into your life.

When you intensify the vitality of the southwestern corner strongly enough, earth luck will work resolutely to help you into a marriage and family situation. You will find yourself meeting or being introduced to someone whose desire to settle down and raise a family to be as strong as yours. I have been flabbergasted at how fast and quickly feng shui can work when it comes to bringing potential husbands and wives together. Only last week I received an e-mail from a very happy young man from Singapore who had found himself a wife soon after energizing his marriage corner. This nice young couple is presently expecting their first child.

Visualizing a partner

Visualize the kind of physical appearance you want in your mate. Clarify how important looks are to you. Does she have to be pretty? Does he have to be tall? Do they need to have good taste in clothes? Are there any physical attributes you find particularly difficult to live with? Are there any habits you could not put up with? The human race has tremendous diversity. It is not possible to think up a composite of the perfect male or female, but is possible to think through the main characteristics that would make you unhappy, annoyed or irritable. Better to undertake a mental listing and be clear on your priorities than be upset later on.

Next it is useful to think through vocal and oral habits that you would prefer to see in your mate or spouse. Do you want someone who is soft spoken and shy or would this sort of person make you very impatient? Do you like someone aggressive and strong? Would you prefer someone who does not talk too much? The attributes of speech, accents, attitudes and nuances of body language play a big part in the attraction equation. Again it is useful to sit down and do some analytical meditation. It will help you to clarify your mind.

Finally, think about what characteristics you would most like to see in terms of attitude, thought processes and motivations in the person you feel will make your ideal mate. These are the three dimensions that make up the substance and manifestations of the mind that define a person's character. Whether or not someone is compatible with you depends on the way he or she approaches the world, how they think and also why they do the things they do and why they think the way they think. Motivations reveal a mountain of information about any person. When you think seriously about these things it will also serve to clarify the sort of person that you are. Analytical meditation of this sort will go a long way towards creating the circumstances of finding a compatible match.

Compatibility with the person you build a home and family with thus lies with you. The circumstances that make these opportunities crystallize can be created and enhanced by feng shui. But by supplementing feng shui with meditative visualization, you will be able to achieve marital status that much faster. Your spouse will also be more in keeping with your own secret aspirations. The result is a higher probability of creating the causes for happiness, and not creating the causes for unhappiness.

Also, strengthening the southwest in this way is very effective for helping couples to conceive. The earth mother energies are made very strong in the southwest when they are strengthened with lights. Not only are lights symbolic of yang energy, they also manifest the fire element which creates earth. These two situations together often create what are known in Chinese as *hei see* or happy occasions. To the Chinese, the three most important *hei sees* in anyone's life are the occasion of marriage, a longevity birthday and a birth.

So if you want to use feng shui to help you find a wife or husband, first, be very certain that getting married will bring you an abundance of happiness. Next, think about the kind of woman who will make you an ideal wife or the kind of guy who represents your ideal husband. Think in terms of body, speech and mind and look to the box on the previous page for help and advice.

Feng shui can also help to dissolve obstacles that might be standing in the way of your happiness. Thus, if the feng shui of your southwest is afflicted by the presence of a frequently used toilet located in that part of the house, then a great deal of your marriage happiness is being flushed away daily. Similarly, if the kitchen occupies the southwest, then the kitchen is pressing down your marriage happiness luck. And if a storeroom is located in that corner, marriage luck turns stagnant and cold. The extent to which these afflictions hurt the marriage (and relationships) happiness of the household depends on the different fate luck of each individual in the household.

If you happen to be going through an astrologically bad time, or if the flying star influences also happen to be bad for the southwest of your house, then the bad luck caused by the afflicted feng shui of the southwest simply becomes more pronounced. Misfortunes associated with failed relationships, quarrels and misunderstandings then become more severe. The annualized flying star number of the southwest afflicts this corner during the years 2001 and 2004. Auspicious annual flying stars for the southwest occur during the years 1999 and 2000. This broad-based reading is usually supplemented by investigating the flying stars for the months and days of the year but is not covered in this book.

Enhancing marriage opportunities

Feng shui offers several different methods of bringing an abundance of love and happiness with someone special. There are very few kinds of aspirations that can match that of finding genuine love and feng shui can very easily increase your chances of getting married if that is what you want.

Mandarin ducks are wonderful symbols of marital togetherness. Place a painting of a pair of these ducks in your bedroom. You can also purchase a pair of ceramic ducks, or a pair of ducks made of crystal or earth-coloured semi-precious stone. Do not use mandarin ducks made of wood as they are not as effective. Ducks that are made of an earth material, or better yet, a semi-precious stone, works in a more powerful way with the element of the southwest, which is earth.

I recommend that you keep a pair of mandarin ducks that are made of red jasper. This is a particularly good stone to use for feng shui symbols of good fortune. The red colour indicates the presence of yang energy. It also reveals the presence of hematite, which the ancient Chinese think of as the most valuable of earth stones.

Hematite contains a sprinkling of iron. It has the deep energy of the earth as well as the sea and it is known to possess powerful energizing qualities. The link between iron and the earth's magnetic field could well be responsible for the seemingly endless supply of energy of the hematite. Combined with quartz it becomes red jasper, a stone which is also rich in healing and protective attributes.

Do not place one or three ducks here. A single duck is a sign of loneliness and sorrow. A single anything always connotes loneliness and it is for this reason that the Chinese almost always display auspicious objects and symbols in pairs. If you keep three ducks you could well have to put up with infidelity and betrayal in your love relationships. Your marriage will get crowded.

Pairs also signify a doubling of happiness. For good marriage luck this doubling attribute becomes a symbol of conjugal bliss. Thus, the Chinese character for double happiness is widely used as a decorative symbol during marriage dinners. Placing this double happiness sign in the bedroom is a powerful energizer of marriage luck.

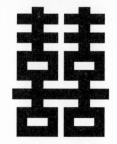

Double happiness
symbol

You can make your own double happiness symbol by tracing and enlarging the symbol shown in the illustration right. Decorate it with flowers and use it as a wall poster. Or place it under glass on your dressing table. The double happiness is a very auspicious sign so that in addition to an abundance of marital happiness it will also attract other types of family luck.

The best way to activate marriage luck, however, is to combine element feng shui with compass formula feng shui. This requires you to do two things simultaneously. First, use the fire element to activate the southwest corner. Place a bright light in this part of your living room or your bedroom. In the cycle of the five elements, fire produces earth. A bright light in the southwest will stimulate the production of the earth element, which enhances the southwest. This, in turn, will cause the opportunities for marriage to be created since the southwest signifies the creation of family.

Secondly, arrange your bed in such a way that you sleep with your head pointed in the direction of your personal nien yen direction. This is the direction that energizes love, marriage, family and good relationships in your life. Even if this means rearranging your bed in a way that does not have it flush with the wall, do it. Try to take your sleeping direction correctly since activating the nien yen is most auspicious in all matters relating to family and social relationships.

In tapping this direction, however, please be mindful of the general feng shui taboos for beds (see pages 90–93). As with all other feng shui recommendations, however, sometimes it is simply not physically possible to arrange furniture and place doors in the most ideal positions and orientations. When confronted with such a situation, you will have to use other methods. This is the reason why I offer different techniques for activating romance and love luck. It is not necessary to do everything suggested here. Often following one technique and method correctly is sufficient.

To find out your personal nien yen direction, work out your personal Kua number (see page 62) and then refer to the table right, which matches the Kua number with the nien yen direction.

Activating for marriage luck alone, however, is insufficient. You need also to ensure that the yin and yang energies of your home or apart-

Discovering your nien yen direction

Kua number	Your nien yen direction
1	south
2	southwest
3	southwest
4	east
5	northwest for men, west for women
6	southwest
7	northeast
8	west
9	north

ment are not generating vibes that are contrary to your aspirations. This means that the male and female energies inside the home should reflect a proper balance.

So in the apartment of a woman who wants to find a husband she must make sure that the apartment does not look too feminine. There should be touches of male energy in the home. If only pictures of women adorn the walls, if all the soft furnishings are frilly and flowery and the whole colour scheme suggests feminine energy exclusively, then the chances of attracting a man's permanent presence in the home would be difficult. In feng shui, opposites do not necessarily attract.

In the same way, apartments that are bachelor pads should not be too male. When there is an absence of female energy, yin and yang is out of sync. The bachelor occupant will find it harder to land a potential wife since his home will not be welcoming to the entrée of female energy.

The best way to design the interior of any bachelor apartment, even if the bachelor girl or boy is not looking to get married, is to have a good mix of male and female energies. When only one gender dominates, the feng shui is out of balance. It cannot be auspicious and marriage/family luck becomes diminished.

Activating the energies of love

The best energizer for a great sex life (especially for the man) is the presence of the *mou tan* flower or peony. The red peony is a symbol of the most exquisite passion. This goes back to the mythical tale of the *mou tan's* association with one of the most famous Imperial concubines in Chinese history. It is said that the legendary Yang Kuei Fei, China's most famous concubine and the favourite of the emperor, enjoyed the secrets of eternal youth and appeal because of her great love of the *mou tan* flower.

Throughout the year, this beautiful flower would be brought to the capital from all parts of China to adorn her suite of rooms and her boudoir in the Imperial palace. The seemingly magical qualities of this flower apparently acted like an aphrodisiac, and it energized the young concubine's premises so much the emperor could neither leave her, nor be satiated. So undivided was the emperor's love for her, and so completely was he in her thrall, he could deny her nothing and in the end it was this obsessive love for his concubine that brought about his downfall. As a result, Yang Kuei Fei's name remains in Chinese history books to this day.

The peony has thus been symbolic of sexual love ever since. Placing the *mou tan* in the home is said to ensure that the young daughters of the household will find good husbands who will love and cherish them the way the emperor cherished his beloved concubine. The peony signifies the young girl in full bloom. In the early years of a marriage, placing the peony in the bedroom is considered good feng shui for the marriage.

In later years, however, when a couple has reached middle age and the children of the household have been born, the peony should no longer be hung in the bedroom. This is because by then, the young wife has become transformed into the earth mother and the peony is no longer a suitable symbol for the marital bedroom. If the peony continues to be hung in the bedroom, it will only energize an abundance of infidelity. The husband will develop a roving eye outside the marriage. While this may have been accepted, and even encouraged in the old days, the situation today is considerably different.

Marital infidelity today will cause unhappiness; infidelity is not in line with the moral expectations. The peony painting should thus be stored away until the young daughters grow up. And when the daughters reach marriageable age, it should be hung in the living room to activate the energies of passionate love, this time for the next generation.

Another excellent way to energize conjugal bliss is to ensure that both husband and wife sleep in accordance to their respective nien yen directions. This makes for an abundance of love in their lives. If the directions of husband and wife are not the same, it is advisable to have two beds, each orientated in the direction that best reflects the nien yen of each person. Again this is not always easy to do since most bedrooms are too small to accommodate two beds. If this is the case then sleeping with the bed orientated in accordance to the husband's nien yen direction will be the solution.

If such a solution offends the sensitivities of my women readers they can do what I do. My husband and I belong to different groups in terms of auspicious compass directions and the directions that bring me luck cause him problems and vice versa. In the early days I followed the above advice and slept in accordance with my husband's nien yen direction, and this energized our family luck. It was one of the methods we used to activate my husband's descendants luck. But now, many years later, we each have our own beds and bedrooms. As a result we both enjoy an abundance of wonderful luck in many different aspects of our lives, including having a great love life.

Special advice for women

I always remind my married women friends that feng shui is an ancient Chinese science and as such, much of feng shui guidelines and principles are geared towards making the family patriarch successful, rich, happy and living to a ripe old age. One other thing feng shui does for any household is to ensure many healthy sons to carry on the family name. Feng shui also ensures no shortage of concubines for the family patriarch. As such many of the techniques for creating prosperity for the family also implicitly create many wives and sons.

Success for families in the traditional context was often measured not only in terms of the patriarch's wealth, position or prominence but also by the number of secondary wives and concubines there were in his household. Like the emperor, men of position in old China often had an entire harem of wives!

In the context of the modern environment, therefore, I want to offer special feng shui advice for my married women readers. In activating the luck of your home to attract wealth and prosperity you must also be aware of the hidden dangers. You must also make sure you are not energizing for your husband to have a roving eye, or worse leave the family roost altogether and get himself another wife. Feng shui, which is originally designed to attract wealth and prosperity into the home, can sometimes inadvertently cause infidelity in a marriage.

Firstly, do be careful about water features. These are wonderful for activating prosperity luck, especially when you use water features like waterfalls, aquariums and small fish ponds. However, do be careful that in building these ornamental water features you place them correctly. For example, you must make certain that you do not place water features on the right-hand side of your main door. This will cause the man to develop love interests outside the marriage. The right-hand side is taken to mean the right side of you as you stand at the door facing outwards.

Instead, the water feature must be on the left-hand side of the door. This guideline applies equally whether your water feature is inside or outside the door. Water features in the vicinity of your front door always bring more wealth if the locations happen to coincide with the east, the southeast and the north part of your whole garden. But if in placing your water features in these three directions, it has to be placed on the right side of your main door, then you should really not have it at all since having prosperity is not much use if you lose your husband! This does not bring abundance, it only creates a lot of unhappiness.

Families with swimming pools should be especially mindful of the location of the pool. If it lies on the right-hand side of the main door (inside looking out) it is indeed highly likely that there will be problems caused by infidelity. Those of you reading this and having water features on the wrong side of the door should either close down the water feature or change the location of the door.

Secondly, be very careful about the features you have in the bedroom. I have already warned you about hanging a painting of peonies in the bedroom or, indeed, a painting of any kind of flowers. Flowers in the bedroom signify the presence of plenty of women in your life – like the old days when one man had many wives and concubines. So do not agree to hang pictures of flowers, or have so-called artistic pictures of nude women in the bedroom. If your husband insists, hang these paintings in the study or another part of the home, but not in the bedroom.

More about mirrors

More important than the presence of flowers is the presence of mirrors that directly reflect the conjugal bed. The effect of mirrors, or any reflective surface which face the bed, is that the marriage will be disturbed by the presence of a third party. There will be danger of infidelity, and this can be on the part of either one of the married couple (see also page 92). If the mirror in your bedroom does not reflect the bed, it does not cause problems. Hence mirrors which are placed on the same wall as the headboard of the bed are usually acceptable and do not cause feng shui problems.

Mirrors and other reflective surfaces such as TV screens can also cause couples to be separated for long periods of time. This does not necessarily mean only divorce or separation as in the breakup of a marriage. These can be separations caused by business and work commitments. If you want your husband not to have to go on business trips excessively, and if you want to make sure your marriage is not disturbed by a sweet young thing targeting your husband, you should remove all mirrors that directly face the bed.

Mirrors placed inside cupboards and shut from view when the cupboard doors are closed do not have this negative effect. As already discussed on page 92, mirrors that are covered by curtains also do no harm. But mirrors that reflect the bed from the ceiling create a great deal of mischief in any marriage or serious relationship.

8 An abundance of good family luck

*'Luck cannot be said
To be auspicious when one has
no family.'*

IN THE CHINESE pattern of life and living, there can be no meaning to a man's life when he is not part of a family. This is the ultimate unit around which society and state evolves. The family represented, and in many ways continues to represent, the traditional focal point of success and aspirations. It is the honour of the family name around which affluence and abundance are defined.

In many feng shui definitions of prosperity, therefore, family well-being, family name and family descendants feature as significant attributes. Luck cannot be said to be auspicious when one has no family, or when the family name is sullied in any way, or when one has no male descendants to carry on the name. Indeed, there can be no greater misfortune than when a family's name dies with a last male descendant. It is for this reason that in families that have no male heirs, the matriarch almost always adopts a male heir.

Feng shui directly addresses the family as a unit. Thus the Pa Kua's eight sides are allocated to a family with six children: three sons and three daughters. The place of the father is the northwest while that of the mother is always the southwest, a corner that always benefits from the efforts of the women of the household.

The eldest son of the family is identified with the east, which is the corner that symbolizes growth and development. In the Forbidden City in Beijing you will see that the young princes of the Imperial family had their quarters built in the east wing of the palace complex. This is the place of the wood element and the corner always benefits from the presence of healthy growing plants.

The place of the eldest daughter is also the corner of wood, but this time it is small wood. This is the southeast, which is also symbolic of growth and development. The trigram of this corner is *sun*, which represents the wind. The two corners east and southeast are the corners most vividly connected to young children of the family. Until they are well into their teens the children of a family will thrive in this part of the home.

Activating the luck of the family patriarch

The place of the father or family patriarch is associated with the northwest. Here the trigram symbol is *chien*, which is three solid lines, the most yang corner of the house. This part of the home is the most important for the family since the luck of the patriarch in many ways affect the luck of the entire family. He is the breadwinner and his fortunes determine the fortunes of the family.

When this northwest corner of the house is missing, the luck of the patriarch (and by extension, the family) is seriously curtailed. Luck associated with the advancement of careers and enhancement of incomes for him will be missing and this translates into a desperate lack of opportunities. Sometimes when the northwest corner is missing, the family will lack the presence of a patriarch and this can also mean that he is either away a great deal on business or he has set up another home elsewhere and has a second 'family'. A missing northwest corner is therefore a serious feng shui affliction. Priority should be given to correcting this situation. There are several reliable methods to do this.

Using a mirror

Use a wall mirror to visually 'extend' the missing northwest corner. This should only be done if the wall is either part of the living room or dining room. And it will be doubly auspicious if the mirror can reflect activity, which lends precious yang energy to what I term the 'pretend northwest corner'. If you use a mirror in this way, make sure that it covers the entire wall. Do not allow the feet or heads of residents to be cut off by having a mirror that is too small or too low. Also do not use mirror tiles that create breaks in the images reflected. In fact, mirror tiles are usually bad news anywhere in the house (even in bathrooms) and it is best not to use them at all.

It is also necessary to ensure that the mirror that you fix on the wall does not reflect the main front door as this causes good luck that enters the home to flow right out again. It should also not reflect a staircase. If it reflects a staircase going up, luck dissipates into 'nowhere' and if it reflects a staircase that is going down, luck descends and disappears. At the same time, also make sure that it does not reflect a toilet since this has the effect of creating a toilet in the north-west corner, a situation which also creates bad luck for the patriarch.

Using wall mirrors to correct a missing corner is thus not always possible. If the missing corner lies in the vicinity of the bedroom, you cannot have a wall mirror installed since this could be reflecting your bed (see pages 92 and 125). If any of the above scenarios describe your situation, the conclusion is that you may not be able to resort to using a wall mirror to correct your missing corner.

Installing bright lights

A second solution for a northwest missing corner will be to install very bright lights in the missing corner. This will be easier to install if you have a garden. Try to regularize the shape of your home by having a tall and bright light installed in the corner. Let the light be placed fairly high up – as high as the height of the house itself. This has another auspicious effect since the tall light also creates good yang energy for the corner.

If you don't have a garden or it is not possible to install a bright light in the garden, you can use a wallpaper to create a visual extension to the wall with the missing corner. This is a very effective way of 'extending' the wall and I have seen some imaginative and very effective 'extensions' done in this way. If you cannot find suitable wall-paper, you can also hang a large painting or print which suggests a courtyard or garden scene. A wallpaper with proper perspectives drawn to suggest three-dimensional scenery painted as one large picture will visually add depth and appear to extend the wall. This sort of effect is very popular with some interior decorators and they are also excellent for enhancing the feng shui of a home. However, this sort of wallpaper can be expensive since it often needs to be custom painted by a skilled craftsperson or artist.

Hanging a wind chime

To enhance the northwest, hang a six-rod metal wind chime in the corner that corresponds to the northwest. You can either consider the whole house in its entirety to locate the northwest or you can use the

---

The value of good fortune symbols

Probably the best method of producing good feng shui for the head of the family is to place a pile of polished decorative stones in the northwest corner. If you like, you can spray some gold paint on the stones to simulate the presence of gold. This is a very good technique since the element of the northwest is big metal, and in feng shui terms, metal is like gold. The pile of stones represents the earth element in which gold is found. In the cycle of the five elements, earth produces gold. The energies created are thus in harmonious balance.

To give added strength to the use of symbolic feng shui, strongly visualize the stones as 'gold in the place of heaven' when you are setting them up. This is because the trigram of the northwest (chien) also represents heaven. Be very relaxed in your expectations of success. There is no need to take an overly serious attitude towards the placement of the good fortune symbols. However, it is also not necessary to be frivolous.

Feng shui is not a spiritual practice that requires faith for its potency to take effect. You do not have to believe in it for feng shui to bring you good luck, or to correct your bad luck. Nevertheless, it is also not necessary to create massive doses of negative energy by being too intense about outcomes.

I am always completely relaxed about the feng shui symbols I use for my home. While doing the placements of these symbols I usually concentrate and focus my energies very strongly, but as soon as the exercise is done, I usually forget about it. I am always confident that my feng shui enhancers will bring my family and me many spurts of wonderful good fortune.

For variety and change I use many different versions of the same symbols. This is because I like the decor of my house to also look good. Besides, I am a great believer in creating good yang energy by moving furniture around every few months. In addition to making me clean out the corners and sweep out the collected dust and dirt of nooks and crevices, it also allows me to purify all the corners of my house with special incense and specific feng shui space clearing techniques.

---

northwest corner of the living room to create enhancing luck. The wind chime is one of the best symbols to use for this corner of the home since it is in perfect harmony with the element of that particular corner.

Placing a metallic bell in the northwest is also an excellent energizer. Bells are a symbol of good reputation and the presence of one in the home brings into being propitious good fortune for the family.

Preventing bad feng shui for the breadwinner

The northwest corner will be afflicted either by the presence of a toilet located in that corner or because the kitchen or storeroom is placed there. You should endeavour to overcome these unfortunate situations in order to reduce or totally remove these causes of bad luck in your home which affect the patriarchal breadwinner. Toilets in the northwest flush down all the luck of the family patriarch. It then becomes necessary to symbolically press down on the negative energies created by the toilet (see page 101).

When the kitchen is located in the northwest, and worse, the stove or cooker is placed here, the effect can be quite disastrous. An open fire used for cooking when placed in the northwest creates a situation of fire at heaven's gate. This is not merely unlucky, it is potentially a tragic and disastrous configuration and you should immediately rearrange the placement of the stove if you have this affliction in your home.

If you do not use a naked flame to cook on, or if the bulk of your cooking is done in an oven where there is no open fire, the situation is not a problem. Then the way to press down on the bad luck caused by the presence of the kitchen will be to use a five-rod wind chime. You can use the same method to nullify the location of a storeroom in this corner.

If the northwest is where the toilet, kitchen or storeroom is located, it is inadvisable to energize the corner with good fortune symbols. Your energizer will simply become negatively affected and the results will bring neither abundance nor happiness.

The place of the matriarch

While it is important to protect the feng shui of the northwest, that of the southwest is also important since the southwest represents the important matriarchal trigram *kun* symbolized by three broken yin lines. This is the place of the mother where the earth element becomes extremely significant. The southwest is said to be the receptacle of all the good family luck for the home. Placing a large ceramic, terracotta or other clay urn here in this corner will allow huge amounts of chi to accumulate and settle. This brings an abundance of extreme good fortune that benefits the whole family because in feng shui, a family's good fortune is said to always flow from the efforts of the matriarch.

Affluent Chinese usually display large decorative ceramic urns or giant vases in the southwest. These have good fortune symbols – flowers or fruits – drawn on them to manifest great good fortune for the family. Such urns are left empty to receive all the good energy that is expected to flow into the urn.

You should not place flowers inside these symbolic receptacles of good fortune. Filling them with flowers suggests the presence of water made excessively yin by the flowers. Keeping them empty attracts chi because when there is a vacuum, it attracts energies.

Some feng shui masters use urns to trap stagnant or killing chi. This is also very effective when you have an afflicted southwest corner. For instance, if you have a toilet in the southwest, the marriage will be affected, and the mother will suffer severe unhappiness.

Usually urns and vases for attracting the good sheng chi are round at the bottom and have a small neck. Such containers also look like vases. Those used for collecting and trapping bad chi have a broader base and mouth.

Personally, I do not like using urns to trap killing breath in the southwest. Since this is an earth corner it is better to use ceramic ware to attract sheng chi – the good dragon's breath.

If the corner is afflicted by the presence of a toilet I prefer to use the Chinese symbols for collecting bad chi and the best symbol to use is the symbolic copper pagoda.

The pagoda is excellent for trapping and keeping shar chi (killing breath) under control.

Hang a metal wind chime with a built-in pagoda design in the toilet to neutralize the bad effect of a toilet. These types of wind chimes made of copper can be purchased at very little cost from Chinese emporiums and supermarkets. Do not hang them with mobiles of fish and other symbols since they are neither appropriate nor effective for pressing down bad luck.

When you have a toilet in the southwest, all the women of the household will suffer problems in their love life. Either the men they go out with will cheat on them, or they are unsuitable to start with. If there are girls of marriageable age in the family, having an afflicted southwest will hurt their chances of getting married. An afflicted southwest will also curtail the marriage opportunities of the sons in the family, or the wives they marry have a hard time fitting in with the family.

Sometimes an ailing southwest corner (caused by the presence of a toilet or when hit by a sharp edge) creates discord among the women of the family. Thus daughters and mothers cannot get along, and sisters living in the same house suffer from incessant misunderstandings. In short, there is a great deal of bickering and disharmony in the home.

If the southwest is being hit by other manifestations of bad feng shui, it will also bring sorrow to the marriage by creating discord between husband and wife. Examples of such manifestations are being at the end of a long corridor, being hit by the edge of two walls meeting, or having heavy exposed overhead beams in the ceiling.

A safeguard against interior poison arrows like these is to strengthen the southwest corner with a pile of boulders tied with red thread.

This reinforces the earth element of the corner and also energizes for good marriage luck, bringing marriage opportunities to unmarried sons and daughters. The presence of well-energized boulders also creates circumstances that lead to happier marriages to those already married.

Indeed, when the southwest corner has good feng shui, the entire family will enjoy harmony and happiness. If placing boulders is a problem, you can use anything that can represent the earth element. Thus a painting of a mountain is an excellent substitute, or you can use a cluster of natural quartz crystals. Alternatively, place a globe in the southwest since this symbolizes the earth itself.

Enhancing techniques for the southwest are best supplemented with lights. My personal favourite is the crystal chandelier since this signifies a doubling of the abundance of earth. I never allow myself to forget the most fundamental underpinning of feng shui: the luck of the earth, as opposed to luck from heaven or luck that we create for ourselves. The Chinese believe these three types of luck cast equal influences over the direction and quality of our life.

When energizing feng shui therefore, we are energizing for earth luck and as such the earth element is especially important. Lights (fire element) create crystals (earth). In fact, crystals (whether natural or man-made) represent the wealth of the earth and are considered to bring good luck almost anywhere you place them. But they bring extra special potency when placed in the southwest corner because this is the place of big earth. The other two earth sectors of the home are the northeast (small earth) and the centre of the home.

If you like, you can display natural quartz crystals on a table in the southwest. If you tie a red thread around the crystal it will energize all the potent energies of the crystal. This is because the red thread creates yang energy, thereby activating it.

Activating family luck

When the southwest enjoys good feng shui, the family usually exists in a state of harmony. Husbands and wives live with few conflicts. Sibling differences and rivalry will be non-existent. There is a great deal of family happiness and a sense of togetherness. This brand of abundance is often far more blissful and satisfying than the abundance of material wealth.

Family luck means that the family plays and stays together. It also means that members of the family stay loyal and are committed to each other. To enhance this kind of good fortune, it is important to take care of the feng shui of the centre of the house.

This area is said to represent the family's relationship luck with each other, and the best rooms to locate here are either the family or dining room. When the centre of the house is the place where the family gathers at the end of each day, it means that the heart of the home is filled with happy yang energy. There is life and love and happiness. Eat at the centre of the home and play at the centre of the home. When the heart is pumping along happily everything else has good feng shui.

Energize the centre of the home by magnifying the presence of the earth energy. Place a crystal chandelier here to create wonderful good fortune. Do not have a staircase in the centre of the home, and especially not a spiral staircase, which will symbolize a deadly, corkscrew boring into the heart of the home. The result of such a feature is usually very tragic. If you have such a spiral staircase, try to change the staircase altogether. Move it to the side of the house and if you cannot do this, at least fill up the empty spaces in between the steps. Otherwise the wealth of the family simply flies out the window!

Sweeping circular staircases have the same effect when they are in the centre of the home. I know of several very rich friends who, carried away by their new wealth, built palatial homes with wide, sweeping circular staircases that were not just placed in the centre of the home, they also directly faced the main door. These staircases made for the grand entrance but it is sad to say that every one of them have been adversely and severely affected by the Asian economic crisis. The circular staircase in the centre of the house is truly dangerous. Curved staircases are good feng shui but these too should be by the side and not in the centre of the home.

While on the subject of staircases, do remember not to (under any circumstance) place a red carpet on circular staircases, especially those located in the centre of the home. In this situation, the red will symbolize blood and again this is a feature which leads to great tragedy and unhappiness for the family.

The toilet, kitchen or storerooms should never occupy the centre of the home. Toilets that are located here create the most amounts of shar chi for the family. This is a very unlucky layout. It not only drains the wealth and assets of the family, it also causes a great deal of unhappiness and misunderstanding. When you have a toilet in the centre of the home, you will create a feeling of deprivation because the energies of the home are simply drained away. More, the toilet flushes away the luck of the family. You should correct this arrangement quickly by removing the toilet or stop using it altogether. If you cannot remove the toilet see page 101 for ways to help counteract all that yin energy.

The centre of the home, however, is an ideal place to hang a happy family portrait. Every member of the family should be included in the picture and everyone should look happy, well-dressed and successful. The patriarch should always be seated and the matriarch should be decked out with the family jewels. The general idea is to create an aura of abundance, and to present a lasting impression of a happy successful family that is whole and complete. Creating this sort of imprint in the centre of the home produces wonderful energies that keep the family safely together.

It also ensures that the family continues to be close despite the children having grown up and living in their own homes. It will create the cause for frequent family get-togethers and reunions. No matter how far away the children of the family fly off to, to study or work, they will always return home if you hang a happy full family portrait in the centre of the home. They will also keep in touch with each other and siblings will get along famously. Family portraits should include only the immediate family of the patriarch.

How the family members pose for the portrait also has feng shui significance. I have a great fondness for the triangular shape with the most important member of the family placed at the apex of the triangle. This shape is symbolic of the fire element and manifests yang energy. Fire is also the element of the south, which in turn signifies honour and a good name. The triangular shaped arrangement of the family portrait thus manifests this kind of luck. However, it is also possible to create water element seating arrangements to manifest wealth luck or wood element symbolism to create growth luck. Water element is a wavy shape while wood element is rectangular.

Family activities like watching television and playing card and other games create excellent feng shui energy when they take place in the centre of the home. This is because family activity creates yang intensity and when the heart of the home is flush with yang energy, it produces excellent family feng shui.

€nergizing descendants luck

Feng shui offers excellent hope for childless couples. If you want children but have been having a hard time conceiving or finding a child to adopt, perhaps there might be something in your home creating blocks and obstacles to your overall descendants luck. This is what happened to my husband and me. For many years we tried hard to start a family with no luck until it reached a stage when we gave up hope altogether. We had been to see so many doctors and tried every every recommendation yet we were unsuccessful until one day my kung fu teacher, Mr Yap Cheng Hai, who was also an expert on feng shui, came to our home and diagnosed the problem of our childlessness.

Mr Yap told us that several features in our beautiful home were conspiring to bring us bad feng shui. Firstly, our main door was made of glass (this is a big feng shui taboo). Secondly, directly in front of our house was a gigantic casuarina tree, which was sending the most horrendous luck to us. Thirdly, the staircase of the home was directly facing the entrance. There was little we could do about these three major feng shui afflictions in our house.

In the end we moved out of that house and built our own home. It took three years to do this and in the interim, my husband and I split temporarily. The old house had also been disastrous for our marriage. When we got back together again the new house was ready. Mr Yap had helped us to design the house in such a way as to energize our descendants luck.

In designing the layout of the new house, we chose the corner that corresponded to my husband's nien yen direction to be the location for our bedroom (see page 123), and to further energize his descendants luck, the bed was oriented to ensure that his head was also pointed to his nien yen direction. According to Mr Yap when it comes to children luck, it is the husband's descendants luck that must be energized, not the wife's. This feng shui method for conceiving can only work, of course, if there is nothing medically wrong with either husband or wife.

Mr Yap had also suggested that if we wanted to have a son we could also place a pair of ceramic elephants inside our bedroom, on either side of the door. He explained that this was an old Chinese belief in that the precious elephant was a symbol of fertility for male children. Since I secretly wanted a girl and my husband did not mind either way, I decided to let nature take its course. Besides, at that time I only half believed that feng shui could work. To our delight, Jennifer was conceived four months after we moved into our new house.

She was born in the tenth year of our marriage, which at that time was extremely shaky, but with her arrival, our relationship took a turn for the better. Today it is 21 years later and we continue to live in this same house. It is now considerably enlarged as our fortunes have progressively improved and our feng shui has also been systematically refined as my knowledge has expanded. Our daughter is grown-up now and our family continues to stay together despite many ups and downs.

Feng shui did not help only me to start a family. Energizing descendants luck has also brought a great deal of happiness to many of Mr Yap's clients over the years. He has told me that if the couple having the problem have something medically wrong with one of them, energizing descendants luck will help them to find a suitable baby for adoption.

According to many Chinese feng shui books, the bedroom of the emperor in the Forbidden City is always decorated with paintings of a hundred children to symbolize fruitful unions that will lead to many princes. This was to ensure that the Imperial line was not short of male heirs to the throne. Placing pictures of babies in the conjugal bedroom is thus believed to activate this symbolic method of creating children's luck.

Feng shui for your children

There are different ways of energizing good fortune for your children. From birth until they become teenagers, children benefit from being placed in rooms on the east side of the home. The east is the place of growth and children benefit from this aspect of their surroundings. They will enjoy good health and grow up sturdy and strong. If you want them to grow up with a sense of family, and to identify with the family's aspirations for them, you should let them sleep with their heads pointed to their individual nien yen direction.

In addition you can energize their education luck by placing a small crystal globe in the northeast of the bedroom. It is not necessary to do anything else save to ensure that there are no mirrors in the bedroom, and to observe all the basic feng shui guidelines already spelt out so far.

When your children reach their teen years, you might want to give them a desk as well. Orientate the desk to let them study while directly facing their auspicious growth direction (see pages 63–4). This direction is especially potent for energizing education luck.

In addition, hang a wind chime in the west side of the bedroom but make sure that in doing so you do not hang the wind chime directly over the bed. If the wind chime can be hung near the window it will be excellent. A seven-rod wind chime is best for this but if this is not possible then a six- or eight-rod wind chime will do just as well. Hanging these wind chimes will create excellent luck for those who want or need financial assistance to further their tertiary education. Those in need of scholarships should hang a seven-rod wind chime.

Creating harmony

The application of feng shui to create a state of harmony in the home requires a comprehensive knowledge of good fortune symbols. Also required is a proper understanding of the five elements and their interactive effect on each other. By dividing the whole space in the home into eight corners and a centre, feng shui energizers can be used to create harmony for the home. Each one of the corners corresponds to one of the compass primary and secondary directions and each direction has a house element. To enhance the harmony and luck of each corner, augment the element of that corner and raise its energies. This is most efficiently done through the use of objects that signify good luck.

The practice of feng shui involves choosing these objects carefully. Look at the table below, which offers vital clues and suggestions for creating harmony in each of the corners. Study the table carefully and start energizing each corner of the living room of your home by following the guidelines given.

Energizing corners

Direction	north	south	east	west	northwest	northeast	southwest	southeast
Element	water	fire	wood	metal	metal	earth	earth	wood
Season	winter	summer	spring	autumn	autumn	between seasons	between seasons	spring
Shape	wavy	triangle	rectangle	round	round	square	square	rectangle
Good luck	fountain	lights	plants	bells	coins	stones	hills	plants
Objects	birdbath bowls	candles sounds	flowers bamboo	chimes stereo	gold	crystals globe	boulders urns	flowers bamboo
Colour	blue black	red orange	green brown	white metallic	white metallic	yellow ochre	beige earth	green brown

Take a systematic approach towards the creation of harmony in the home. To start with please note I am suggesting that you energize only the living area of your home. Do not mess around with the bedrooms. The bedroom is a place of rest and a different perspective must be taken when taking action on the feng shui of bedrooms. The table opposite should therefore be closely followed for the living areas of the home only: the living room, dining room and family room.

In implementing the suggestions for each of the walls of the room, you can use colours to energize one corner, shapes to energize another, and a decorative object for yet a third. It is not necessary to use everything I suggest. Apart from it being impractical and expensive, feng shui also does not work on the basis that more is better. Everything suggested in this book should be done in moderation.

One water feature is sufficient to activate the luck of water. When there is too much water, it will symbolically drown you. Just like if you put too much yang energy and have too many lights, the excess of fire will burn you. Feng shui works best when you make sure that balance is maintained at all times.

In the north

You can create harmony by having blue curtains on your windows, blue carpets on your floors or blue drapes to cover unsightly views outside the house. Any shade of blue will be fine since this is the colour associated with water. In addition, you can incorporate water motifs in your decoration of this north corner or wall. Anything that is wavy or resembles a wave breaking on the seashore can symbolize water.

The north is also the place of the black tortoise. I always recommend people keep a single tortoise in the north. The number of the north is one, so a single tortoise is said to be most auspicious. Do not worry about the tortoise being lonely. There is no such sentiment crossing his head. Invest in a large, wide-brimmed ceramic water container: get one of those decorative containers with auspicious symbols painted on them for good luck.

If you like, you can display a fake tortoise, but do place it inside a shallow water bowl. In this way, you are creating harmony and good fortune with both the water and the tortoise. As the tortoise is also a symbol of longevity and protection, having a single tortoise in your home is often sufficient to ensure you of excellent good fortune all through your career.

Another excellent feature for the north is a large decorative aquarium where you can keep an odd number of arrowanas, goldfish or carp. In an aquarium I always prefer the arrowana. Japanese carps or koi are best kept in a pond created in the ground outside in the garden. Do not place these water features directly under a staircase since water under the staircase hurts the second-generation, the children of the household.

In the south

Here you should energize fire since this is the house element of the south. Place a triangular-shaped piece of furniture or a painting of a cone-shaped mountain. If there are curtains here try to have them in any shade of red. If you are using wallpaper on a south wall, a dominantly red design will attract huge good fortune and harmony for the family. The number of the south is nine so placing nine lights in this part of the room is excellent. Another excellent feature here that is extremely harmonious for the family is the fireplace.

It is also necessary to keep this part of the room well lit. If the door is placed here, it can be painted red to attract precious yang energy.

The celestial creature associated with the south is the crimson phoenix. This is the winged bird that brings enormous opportunities for advancement. Place a beautiful bird – a crane, a flamingo, a rooster or a peacock – to simulate the vitality of the celestial phoenix. I keep three of these birds (made of molded plaster and marble) in the south side of my garden. You can also have these decorative birds inside the house.

A very dear friend of mine was presented with a limited edition crystal phoenix that had flakes of gold inside its body, and it brought enormous good fortune to him. Soon after he displayed it inside a cabinet arranged in the south side of his hall, he was invited to become the Chairman of a large bank. Since then, his fortunes have escalated and he continues in this position in a non-executive capacity even though he is already in his seventies.

In the east and southeast

These directions are the places of the wood element. Here anything that is green or blue creates instant harmony of elements. Place plenty of flowers and live plants in this part of the room since this symbolizes growth. The shape of this corner will be rectangular and the numbers here are three and four. So three potted plants in the east and four vases of flowers in the southeast should bring material wealth and abundant growth opportunities to the family.

The east is also the place of the green dragon so if you can find a beautiful painting or ceramic sculpture of a dragon, placing it in this corner will bring enormous good fortune.

In the west and northwest

Here the ruling colour is white or metallic. Curtains, fabrics, carpets and wallpaper – all the soft furnishings, should have a touch of gold to bring out the auspicious energy of this corner. The best energizer of these corners, however, are the old antique coins of the last dynasty of China. Many superstitious Chinese business tycoons hang the ten emperor coins tied up with red string on the west wall of their office.

You can use coins for the west wall of your house and they can be tied in a variety of lucky ways. The simplest is to tie three coins into a triangle with the yang side up. The yang side is the one with four Chinese characters. The yin side has only two characters. Tied with red string, place these coins inside small jade containers, which are in turn placed inside cabinets.

In the northeast and southwest

The dominantly auspicious colour in these areas will be yellow, ochre or anything that suggests the earth. It can thus be red, which is the colour of fertile laterite soil. Or it can be the yellow of clay or the white of sand . . . or the transparent colour of crystal. In these earth corners anything of the fire element is also auspicious since fire produces earth.

So in this part of the room you can create a warm ambience suggestive of the harvesting period just after summer. If your windows are located here, use curtains that complement the feel of autumn with bright oranges and ochre tones predominating. If the main door is located in either of these two corners, you can once again paint it red for good luck and harmony. If the door is placed in this part of the room, then the colours of summer and autumn will attract wonderful auspicious energy into the home.

Protecting the conjugal bed

There can be no family luck if the two most important members of the family – the father and the mother – do not get along well to the extent that there is physical separation or violence. This is regarded as very severe bad luck, and is often caused by the feng shui of the conjugal bed being adversely affected by bad feng shui. It is therefore important to protect the conjugal bed and make sure it is not being hit by secret poison arrows.

Placement of the bed

An auspiciously oriented bed will have the man of the family sleeping with his head pointed in his most auspicious direction based on the eight mansions formula (see pages 58–63). He will have four good directions to choose from and depending on what kind of luck he wishes to activate, the bed and bedroom can be oriented accordingly. However, not everyone can orientate the bed to exactly fit a given direction. Often there are simply too many obstacles standing in the way.

This is because in orienting the bed according to a certain direction, you could well be hit by any number of harmful features. Thus the bed could be directly facing the door, or placed between two doors, under a window or under a beam – any of which will instantly spoil the feng shui of the bed. So, before reorienting the bed, take a good look at the bedroom itself and see the guidelines given on page 91 for good bedroom feng shui.

9 An abundance of material possessions

'Feng shui
starts from the premise
that the Universe is
plentiful and abundant.

Programme yourself for prosperity and
feng shui will create the
cause and conditions
to actualize it all for you.'

Y OUR USE of feng shui to create prosperity will be considerably amplified if you start from the premise that the Universe in which we all live is a totally plentiful and abundant place, and that everyone in it is entitled to a lavish share of what the Universe can provide. Everything that your heart and mind desires on the material plane and on the emotional, mental and ultimately spiritual levels can be yours for the asking.

Everything you need and want can become part of reality, part of your world, and part of your space. The easiest dreams to achieve are the goodies of the physical plane where money, wealth and prosperity represent the sum total of material aspirations. When the mind generates the determination, and the surrounding environment is made beneficial and accommodating through feng shui, affluence comes enticingly within reach. I often tell people that of all the aspirations offered by the promise of feng shui, it is promise of material abundance that is probably the easiest to achieve.

Feng shui offers many formulas for arranging the living space and designing your rooms so that you can become richer and richer. There are a multitude of methods aimed specifically at increasing incomes and prosperity levels. Feng shui adopts an almost relaxed attitude towards recommendations for improving income levels. The difficulty sometimes arises when you are unsure which technique will suit you best.

Irrespective of whether you use the formula method or fill your home with all the good fortune wealth symbols, you should also attune your mind and your expectations towards the positive outcome. Before you can become seriously wealthy you have to convince yourself that you deserve to become rich.

Convincing yourself is called prosperity programming, and this is the direct opposite of poverty programming: the belief that life is, and should be, full of suffering, the belief that we cannot have everything, that we cannot have our cake and eat it too! I have often asked what on earth I would do with a cake if I could not eat it?

When I was young I was often puzzled by the way my aunts and uncles would chide me for being greedy. I was made to feel guilty for ordering juice instead of water, for preferring to wear lace instead of linen. I was to feel bad for wanting to have it all. For a very long time I believed I was greedy, and allowed myself to be weighed down with this heavy baggage. Then, when I was 22 years old, I discovered Helen Gurley Brown and *Cosmopolitan*. I embraced her want-it-all attitude and almost instantly adopted her philosophy of life. I proceeded to shed all my feelings of guilt for wanting to become rich and successful. For the first time I admitted to myself (without feeling bad about it) that I enjoyed life's little luxuries. I enjoyed having my first car. I loved it when I got my first pay cheque and decorated my first home. When I started working, I enjoyed being financially independent.

It was this release of what I term my childhood poverty programming that enabled me in later life to tell my feng shui mentor Mr Yap Cheng Hai, that it was wealth that interested me. Indeed, at that time, I was only interested in the get rich part of feng shui. Mr Yap explained to me that all material things have an energy field of their own. Because material things are inanimate, he said, their energy fields are more yin than yang. To attract these beautiful things – cars, houses, jewellery, art and so forth – into the home, all we needed to do was to attract or create the precious yang energies of abundance into our homes. The yang energy field would then act as a magnet to attract material comforts and wealth objects into our lives.

Put another way, we can use the science of feng shui to attract large quantities of the cosmic chi or dragon's breath, and with it would come great wealth and prosperity.

Like the New Age enthusiasts, who emphasize the great power of the mind, feng shui also believes in this power. In addition, feng shui contends that there is natural abundance inside the earth. The intrinsic state of the living environment is that it is filled to brimming with nutritious and nourishing prosperity. What you need to do to participate in the earth's abundance and prosperity is to skillfully create channels of energy flows or conduits that direct the prosperity into our lives and living space.

Creating prosperity with feng shui can thus be a breeze – easy and fun. It is not necessary to try everything and every method. Do not let yourself become confused and irritated with the vast amounts of (often) conflicting advice you will be getting the moment you go out looking for feng shui 'masters'. Use your common sense and intelligence to make good judgements about so-called feng shui experts. Do not believe the rubbish that feng shui masters need to live frugally to explain their lack of wealth or indebtedness. Do not buy the tale of the feng shui ascetic, or the feng shui medium, or the feng shui spiritualist. Feng shui experts can be anyone who possess an authentic store of practical and theoretical knowledge. Also, you do not require special amulets or holy objects to enhance your feng shui or to bring you wealth.

Two years ago when I gave a seminar in Melbourne I was told a horror story. In my audience, a 27-year-old young man described how he had paid $9,000 dollars to study under a feng shui 'master'. He was asked to fast for two weeks, go on a feng shui tour of China's feng shui places and part company with his money before he could be taken as a disciple of the master. In your enthusiasm, do not engage just anyone and give him/her the freedom of your own private space.

Feng shui is rich with philosophy and techniques. It is neither a religious nor a spiritual practice although, yes, we can combine our own spiritual practices with feng shui. This is especially the case in the area of space purification. Simple feng shui is very easy to apply to your living and work space and it is no less potent than advanced feng shui. If you want to create prosperity in your life simply start by believing you deserve and want prosperity and then go through the rest of this chapter for some of the things you can do to energize your own wealth luck.

Make new space for new possessions

Before you start changing your furniture around and re-orientating your door, it is useful to first go through your home with a keen eye for all the things you do not need. If you are going to enhance your feng shui to attract new possessions and wealth, you must first make sure there is room inside your home to accommodate the new items. Unless you create space for them, they cannot come into your home.

Start by making room in the physical area of your home. Collect all the clothes, books and paraphernalia of your life accumulated since forever and which you no longer need or want, and give them away immediately. I do this once a year and have been doing it for the last thirty years of my life. I work on the assumption that unless I am prepared to throw out my old possessions with no sense of loss or attachment, I will have no room for the new. I try not to have any emotional attachment to my material possessions, not even the companies I built or acquired. Once I made the decision to cash out, I would sell out to the first good offer I received.

This is a very important preliminary part of the prosperity equation. If you want to become rich you must learn to let go and move with the flow of energy. Feng shui contends that the rhythms of energy that control the creation of monetary luck and bring material things into existence in the Universe suggest constant movement and flow. To appreciate the secrets of prosperity luck and manifestation, we must understand the nature of this rhythm, this flow. For this reason, even as we energize our living space and orientate our homes to tap into good feng shui, we must simultaneously create the inner vacuum to receive prosperity goodies.

Learn to give. It is not clutter you need to throw out and cleanse. It is the mind that needs to be transformed. To receive prosperity you must understand that the more we give, the more we shall receive. The more we give, the larger will be the inner space we will be creating so there is room for yet more things to flow towards us. If we succumb to foolish tendencies to cling on to everything we have and presently own, we will, in effect, be creating blocks on the natural flow of energy in the Universe. We will then be upsetting the rhythms.

When you apply feng shui principles it is useful to remember that feng shui is about manipulating the cosmic chi, and this is akin to the energy of the environment. Energy comes in any form. It can be material wealth, love, affection, recognition, appreciation, money, friendships – it can be anything at all. Auspicious cosmic chi has a tendency to gravitate towards those who have a relaxed attitude towards their aspirations and their ambitions. If you know how to let go and open your arms to receive prosperity, feng shui will work better and faster for you.

If, on the other hand, your attitude is tensed and grasping, even the most auspicious chi entering your home could well turn sour. Look around at the people who make up your world – your friends, colleagues, and members of your family. You will notice that those people who tend to have a grasping attitude are seldom happy. They wear a constant expression of being deprived, desperately trying to grab at whatever is available. Such people are usually stingy, even with their praise. They find it hard to compliment others. They do not know how to outflow, to give, and as a result they have no space in their inner being to receive. Their demeanour generally reflects the starved look. They are full of deadly killing energy and there is insufficient yang vitality inside them.

On the other hand, the generous hearted, those who possess benevolent attitudes, are usually happy, well-adjusted individuals. These sort of people will benefit the most and the fastest from feng shui. They are often the first to praise and offer congratulations, to express their appreciation or to extend sympathetic shoulders. Generous souls exude an aura that is very yang indeed. Such people have plenty of inner space to receive all the prosperity and abundance that good feng shui brings.

If you want feng shui to work its special brand of magic, bear this in mind. Giving generates a really auspicious aura. The more you develop your capacity to give, the more you will be enhancing your personal aura and energy. This is what will attract a truly huge abundance of material wealth.

Visualize everything you want

In addition to generating the inner space to receive prosperity luck, you can also use the power of your own consciousness to strongly visualize all that you want feng shui to bring for you. The wonderful thing about material wealth is that it can actually be quantified. I remember when I wanted to retire at the end of the eighties and was planning to sell all my assets in Hong Kong to return home to Malaysia, I made a mental note of how rich I had to be. I visualized what I needed very strongly and each time I fed my feng shui fish – my arrowana – I visualized myself telling them the magic number.

I had kept five of these living symbols of prosperity in my apartment on the Peak in Hong Kong. My five arrowana were with me for only 18 months but in that short period they did indeed help to bring me enough money to retire for the rest of my life. The use of the arrowana to create wealth luck is a popular practice with Chinese businessmen in the Far East. It works for everyone. The only difference is that it brings different amounts and kinds of wealth to different people. So it is an excellent idea to think about what you want. Focus your mind and give your goals strong energy. Those of you who wish to keep this fish, please note that they feed on live bait. They grow fast and they need a large tank. There is no need to decorate your fish tank – the fish itself are sufficiently mesmerizing. And you really only need a single arrowana. If you want to keep more, stick to odd numbers otherwise the arrowana create friction between you and your friends. You could start quarrelling over money. The arrowana is a tropical fish and during the winter months you might want to keep the water temperature slightly heated. They are not difficult to find and should cost approximately £10 for a 7.5-cm (3-in) specimen. They will grow to about 30 cm (12 in) long within 12 months.

In addition to visualization it is a good idea for you to list the various feng shui energizers you are planning to display in your home. It is not necessary to overdo things, and it is impossible to apply every-thing suggested. Thus you should select only those suggestions that lend themselves to easy practical applications. Use a combination of methods. Often the easiest and most practical recommendations are those that form part of the school of symbolic feng shui (see the table on page 140).

Meanwhile, problems caused by troublesome toilets, missing walls or corners and door orientations often require structural changes. These are usually harder to adjust. Corrective feng shui can sometimes be a source of great aggravation. In such situations, my advice is that you should do what you can and where you really cannot do any-thing about it then use your mind to mentally visualize what has to be done.

Create a mental picture of the way the door should actually be facing. Or build a mental corner into the missing part of the home. In other words, use visualization to assist you in your efforts to create perfect feng shui for your home. When you use the power of your mind in this way, you will be pleasantly surprised how effective it can be.

The mind has the ability to create energy patterns that transform unsuitable orientations and directions. Where necessary, use pictures and drawings to assist in your visualization. This particular method is extremely helpful when dealing with missing corners in the home. When the missing corner is the southeast you know that it affects your wealth luck. It becomes a serious matter. Use your mind to imagine that the missing corner has been filled in.

I had a very good friend, Helen, whose southeast corner was indeed missing. It was a particularly serious missing corner for her because the southeast was also the sheng chi corner and direction for both her and her husband (see pages 88–90). On the face of the preliminary analysis, this suggested that the house would not bring her any prosperity. The first thing I told her to do was to fill in the southeast corner. I also advised her to install a water feature to energize the southeast element of wood, a light to raise the chi of the corner, and to introduce the vital fire element to create the circumstances for the wood element to flower and blossom. This is a very effective way of activating the wood element of the southeast. Although fire burns wood, you must not forget that without the sunlight, plants cannot grow and flowers cannot bloom. Seeds cannot be made and there can be no harvest, so light is very important in the wood corner. But water is important too since without water the plant (symbolizing wood) simply dies.

Helen had a small space in which to work with but she is a determined lady. She strongly visualized a large southeast corner. Then she placed a small fountain in the corner (about 30 cm [12 in] diameter, so you can imagine how small it was) and fantasized it to be very big as well. Finally, she bought some pebbles, sprayed them gold with a can of paint, and she visualized this as real gold.

She asked me if it would work and I congratulated her profusely. Such creativity deserved to be encouraged! Needless to say, Helen went from strength to strength and her business is growing in leaps and bounds. The potency of feng shui can thus be considerably reinforced by the amount of mental energy with which you imbue your efforts. The more committed you are to achieving your goals using feng shui, the faster and more spectacularly it will work.

Those of you who are already veterans at doing visualization will find that when you apply feng shui principles into your living space in this way results will be achieved a great deal faster than for those people who are unable yet to supplement their feng shui practice with this extra dimension. It is because of this that many of the most powerful feng shui masters of olden days in China were monks or temple abbots. Because of their spiritual training in meditation and visualization they were able to enhance their feng shui applications with powerful mental energies. It is probably this aspect of feng shui practice which has given rise to the added dimension of transcendental solutions to difficult feng shui problems expounded by certain other schools of feng shui.

Business feng shui for profits

Feng shui lends itself particularly well to business enterprises, either at the corporate office or mass-market retail store levels. The feng shui of corporate head offices has a huge effect on the fortunes of the company, just as the feng shui of the shop floor will affect the sales turnover and profitability of the shop.

The application of feng shui in business is both exciting and full of promise and corporate profits are affected by mainly two things:

◆ the feng shui of the main door into the office/building
◆ the feng shui of the chief executive's office.

There are good and bad feng shui buildings. I remember about twenty years ago standing in the middle of New York City staring up at the then PanAm building and wondering whether the corporate bigwigs inside this huge company realized they would go out of business one day. I was an MBA student at Harvard at that time and I recall telling my classmate who had come up to New York with me all about feng shui. I pointed to the PanAm building and told him that according to feng shui PanAm would one day cease to exist. A very long avenue that resembled a deadly poison arrow was directly hitting the building.

Corporate buildings should always be designed with great care. Call in the feng shui master at the design stage. Even better, call in the feng shui master before you commit to buying the land since most bad corporate HQ feng shui is due to the presence of killing chi caused by surrounding buildings. It is important to take a defensive approach when planning large real estate projects like office buildings, shopping malls and so forth.

For retailers, the feng shui of the building where you locate your shop will affect your sales. In general, busy areas have better feng shui simply because there is plenty of good yang energy. Such places also tend to be more expensive of course. Those of you who own or manage retail outlets such as restaurants and boutiques might want to study the things outlined below when looking for shop space. There are then several popular and well-tried methods for improving the business feng shui of retail shops.

Good feng shui for shops

- ◆ Avoid shop lots located at the end of a corridor. You will find it tough to generate sales growth. It is worse when you are at the end of a straight road.
- ◆ Avoid shops that share walls with toilets or are placed below toilets on another higher floor. The killing energy is strong!
- ◆ Shops that are deep suggest that you will be in business for a long time. Shops that are shallow suggest you will have a short life span.
- ◆ Shops that have regular shapes are always better than those with irregular shapes.
- ◆ Shops that face a big empty area or a wide corridor are better than those that open into cramped public walkways. The empty area serves as the magical bright hall where auspicious chi settles and accumulates, bringing good feng shui.

- ◆ Shops should never face pillars, columns or sharp objects since these block chi from coming in and also cause secret poison arrows to be produced.
- ◆ Corner shops usually have better feng shui, especially if they are located near the centre of shopping malls. Always choose the corner that has the highest traffic since this corresponds to the place of maximum yang energy.
- ◆ High street shops will benefit from traffic coming from three roads but the shop itself should not face an oncoming road.
- ◆ Traffic should not seem to be flowing away from the shop.
- ◆ A fountain in front of the shop is excellent provided it is not too large in relation to the size of the shop.

Using mirrors

The first method for enhancing feng shui in shops is to use mirrors to line all your display walls. The mirror should also reflect your cash register. Mirrors serve to double customers in the shop and double the cash takings at the end of the day. Shops that use mirrors (especially restaurants) are usually extremely successful if the mirrors are placed correctly.

Do not cut your mirrors into threatening shapes with sharp angles. Simply cover the entire wall with it. Mirrors should not be too low as to visually cut off the heads of tall customers, nor should the feet of customers be cut off. Meanwhile, make sure that the cash register is reflected in the mirror. This will double your sales.

Using Chinese coins

The second method is to tape three special Chinese coins tied with red thread onto the cash register, the cash box or the invoice book. This generates higher income luck. The coins used are antique Chinese coins which have a square hole in the centre. These coins symbolize the union of heaven and earth. There is also a yin side and a yang side. Place the yang side on top.

Make sure you have the red thread in place since this serves to energize the coins. In the event that you find it difficult to find these old Chinese coins, you can also use modern versions of them, or you can use the coins of your own currency.

Some feng shui masters recommend that you hang a sword of coins or the ten emperor coins – these and other variations of coins can be purchased quite easily in the souvenir and antiques shops of Hong Kong, Taiwan, Singapore and wherever else there is a Chinese population. Coins that have been elaborately tied are said to offer both protection against being cheated as well as produce auspicious good fortune for the business. For me, I have discovered three coins tied in a simple manner with the yang side up, is sufficiently powerful as a symbol of good fortune.

Using bamboo

Hang a pair of bamboo pieces tied with red thread high above the cash register. This will create a continuous flow of auspicious chi towards the cash register thereby channelling great good fortune for the shop. The bamboo can be hung up to simulate the Pa Kua shape but as long as the hollow bamboo allows chi to flow through, the effect will be very auspicious. Try to find bamboo that is about 12 mm (1/2 in) in diameter and about 15 cm (6 in) long.

Money feng shui anywhere

Money feng shui tips can be used anywhere – at home, in the shop, at the restaurant, in the factory and in the office. Anyone wanting to use feng shui to enhance their income luck should get a stock of the old Chinese coins since these are excellent money activators. Keep them in your wallet, keep them taped onto important files, even on fax machines and computer monitors. The coins attract money luck. Taping them to the computer will attract money-making ventures via your e-mails and taped onto the fax machine it will bring you loads of opportunities through that machine.

Another excellent method of attracting money luck into your home is to place the God of wealth inside the home. This Chinese representation of an old man sitting on a tiger is known as Tsai Shen Yeh and his presence in the home or office (placed behind you where you sit) is said to bring wonderful money luck. Because the Chinese are rather preoccupied with money, they have more than one wealth God. In fact, the most popular icon deity that symbolizes wealth is the canonized God of war, Kuan Kung. This colourful character features in the classic *The Romance of the Three Kingdoms*. Both deities can be found in any Chinese supermarket.

You can place them in the house near the front door. The energies created by these deities are very auspicious. You do not need to pray to them. They are placed in the home only to symbolize and attract wealth into the house. They are not deities to be worshipped. In addition to these two deities it is also advisable to place the three Star Gods – the Fuk Luk Sau, the God of wealth, prosperity and longevity – in the home. Again these deities are not worshipped. Their presence is meant only to symbolize prosperity and good fortune.

Chinese symbols of prosperity include the celestial creatures – the dragon, the phoenix and the tortoise. When placed inside the house as works of art, these creatures are said to bring good money luck to the family. The tortoise, however, can be real. I have lost count of the number of times I have recommended people to keep a tortoise or its relative (the terrapin) in the house and I am amazed at how wonderfully potent this tip is for so many people. The tortoise brings wealth luck but it also brings good health and longevity. The tortoise is also a symbol of protection. This celestial creature is best placed in the north, and it would be even better if you place it with water because the north is the water element, so placing them together creates a double benefit. If you really cannot have a real tortoise, a fake ceramic one will do just as well.

When you use feng shui symbols as display objects in your home or office it is a good idea to try and place them in accordance with their element significance. When you can get them made in gold, it is a very prosperous symbol. Thus a tortoise that is plated in gold becomes the golden tortoise. Placed in the north the impact is extremely lucky since gold is metal, which produces water.

Another wonderful wealth bringing creature is the three-legged toad. This is a very popular symbol used by Chinese everywhere. The toad has three legs and he is often depicted seated on a bed of coins with the symbol of the yin yang on its back. In its mouth he holds out a coin signifying gold. The three-legged toad is a very lucky symbol. Place him on the floor or on the table near the front door but not directly facing it. This is truly one of the easiest way of energizing money luck. You can place one in each room if you so wish!

A final suggestion regarding the use of wealth symbols is to use the sailing ship. This symbol originated from the old merchant days when the sailing ship represented the arrival of gold and money. Many successful Chinese businesses, especially merchants and traders, used the sailing ship as their logo since this indicated that luck had at last arrived.

Place a model of a sailing ship inside the foyer of your home or office. Make sure the ship is facing inwards, using the direction of the sails to check. The symbolism is that the ship has safely made harbour. Place a few small pieces of real gold on the deck of the ship as this will create much better energy. You may, if you wish, also place pretend gold in the ship, but if you do this you should use strong visualization techniques to lend extra energy.

I have been asked if placing a model of a large cargo airplane inside the foyer has the same effect and I am at a loss to answer since the old books refer only to the sailing ship but not the airplane. Using conventional logic to interpret the reasoning behind the feng shui of the sailing ship I would tend to say yes to the airplane.

Prosperity feng shui for the home

According to the old feng shui masters, a prosperous home is one that nestles in the embrace of the green dragon and the white tiger. This configuration has been described on page 24–5 under landscape feng shui. At a practical level, however, what the old masters are saying is that your home should ideally be located on undulating land where dragons are present. It is only when you live in places where the dragon is present that you can have good money luck. This is one of the basics of feng shui. However, on undulating land you must be very careful that you orientate your front door correctly. Thus you must follow some of these basic rules of feng shui for your home.

1 Land behind your home (this is usually interpreted to mean the opposite of where your front door is located) should always be higher than land in front of your home. If your front door directly faces higher land it is like confronting the mountain. This is a configuration where there can be no prosperity. Worse, such an orientation usually brings enormous bad luck. The best way to

correct this problem is to change your door. No matter how difficult it is, you must try to look for a way of changing the orientation of your home altogether by changing the location of the door. If you cannot, then try hanging a convex yin Pa Kua mirror on the outside wall above the door.

2 Land on the left-hand side of your door (inside looking out) should always be higher than land on the right-hand side. This ensures the dominance of the dragon over the tiger. When the contours of the surrounding land are the other way around, it signifies a situation of danger. To correct such a situation you should install a very tall and bright light on the lower dragon side. This serves to raise the chi of the land that represents the dragon. Another method you can use is to erect a fence on the tiger side and paint it red. The white tiger belongs to the metal element in the Lo Shu grid and red, being representative of fire is able to control the white tiger: fire destroys metal in the cycle of elements.

3 Big water in the form of rivers, lakes and swimming pools should not be behind your home since this makes your home very unlucky. Such a large pool of water behind your home suggests missed opportunities but more than that, it can also be a sign of danger. This will be the case when the land behind you is higher. Water on higher land behind you will cause you to lose all your wealth. It is best to move out of such a house since this is really such an unfortunate configuration.

4 Roads around your house should be studied with care and bad configurations are discussed on page 40. When the road in front of your home is non-threatening and it has two or more feeder roads bringing slow moving traffic towards your house, the effect is most auspicious. This is similar to the flow of good fortune rivers.

5 The best way of ensuring good money luck for the house is to manipulate the positioning of the main door. Then use the eight mansions formula and apply your Kua number. Please refer to the table on page 90 to get your sheng chi direction. Then make certain that your main door is orientated in the direction that represents this direction.

Water feng shui for wealth

In feng shui, water represents wealth and getting the water placement properly and correctly orientated in your home or garden is one of the best ways of creating prosperity luck. At the same time, water should always be applied with care. With the growing popularity of feng shui, landscapes with water features have become fashionable in architectural designs of new buildings. Unfortunately, a little knowledge can be very dangerous since water can be a double-edged sword. Thus, when water flows away from the building or is seen to be flowing outwards the bad luck is very severe. When water flows out, so does money.

In Hong Kong there is a notorious building near the Central Business District known as the Lippo building. It is a building that has such bad feng shui it has seen a long string of its most illustrious (and huge) corporation tenants go bust. Its most recent feng shui victim was the high-flying investment bank Peregrine Investments, and before that the BCCI Banking group, which had its Hong Kong office there. The building has also brought ill fortune to its one-time owners, the Lippo group of Indonesia. The building has bad feng shui because a water feature embraces the building. All around the building there is water, but the water flows outwards, draining all the residents in the building of their money!

There is also a five-star hotel in Singapore that has a large artificial water canal draining the water away from the entrance thereby causing bad feng shui. Needless to say, the hotel has never done well and, in fact, has recently changed owners.

In water feng shui there is a very potent formula that prescribes detailed instructions for the exit direction of water from any home or building. This water formula requires an entire book to explain it, but it is said to be so potent, it has apparently created many of the old tycoons of Taiwan during the immediate post-war period. For our use it is perhaps sufficient that we use an easier water formula that prescribes the placement of water features such as mini fountains, birdbaths and small fish ponds around the home and in the garden.

This formula is based on the flying star formula which indicates that the best locations for these water features from now until the year 2003 are the north, the east, the southeast and the southwest. These are the only four locations in your living room or in your garden where water is auspicious. These four locations continue to be auspicious through to the next twenty-year period which lasts from 2004 to 2023.

10 An abundance of happiness – the bliss of feeling good

'Tune into the soul of your home
Then go for the flow that is auspicious
*   and balanced.*
Let currents of energy
Meander and curve gently and
*   effortlessly.'*

ALL HOMES have their own special brand of energy. There are happy homes and sad homes. Happy homes lift the spirit while sad homes create unease and tension. It is not difficult to tune into the quality of the energies that permeate rooms, houses and places if you consciously focus your mind on feeling the energy of the place.

This means developing sensitivity to the soul of any home – it is a skill that gets better with practice. Give your attention over to any feelings, positive as well as negative, which any space, room or home evokes in you. Follow through with investigations into the background of the place if necessary since this will give you clues as to its quality and attributes. Then take notes of the way the rooms are laid out in relation to each other. Mentally assess the flow and currents of the house. Try to sense if this flow is fast or slow, or simply non-existent. Also count the number of openings – windows and doors – and see if the energy of the home can flow out of them. Become aware of colours and shapes and see if they seem to harmonize in a pleasing way. If anything about the place disturbs you, try to locate the source of your unease.

Dialling into the energies of a home is not all instinct or intuition. I have to say here that I do not subscribe to instinctive or intuitive feng shui – in fact, I really do not think that such a thing exists. If it does, then feng shui cannot be taught since by definition no one can really teach instinct. No one can tell your intuition what to feel or how to feel. I believe that everyone can develop sensitivity to an environment, but this sensitivity is neither your instinct nor your intuition. It is a part of your developed consciousness to the environment.

We can feel that something about a place may not be quite right – that is our consciousness telling us we feel uneasy – but it does not tell us the reason for the feeling of discomfort. To detect what is wrong, and to know how to deal with the problem identified, requires specific space enhancement or feng shui skills and knowledge.

Feng shui is thus a method of diagnosing what is wrong with the arrangements of physical structures in a given space. It is knowing what can be done to improve orientations to improve the flow of energy. This is the substance of feng shui and it is definitely not instinctive. There are correct and incorrect ways of applying feng shui guidelines, but diagnosis has to be made before a cure or cures can be selected.

Before you do this, however, it always helps to investigate the background history of a home. When the house or apartment is new, and the building that previously stood there has been demolished to give way to a modern redevelopment project, you should investigate what was there before they became residential abodes (or offices). Feng shui practitioners always check the provenance of homes and buildings.

If the previous land-use was a hospital, for example, the energy of the entire environment will be extremely yin and probably very sad as well. Hospitals are where thousands of patients passed away in pain, or at least suffered from illnesses. Since old energies created over many years take as long, if not longer – and require special purification techniques to become dissipated or dissolved – you can see why from a feng shui perspective, houses built on land previously occupied by a hospital are not recommended.

In London's fashionable Kensington area there is an extremely pretty block of apartments that has risen from the rubble of a hospital. This redevelopment project is very elegant indeed. But I know of at least three families who have developed serious illnesses or suffered severe losses after moving into this very expensive apartment block.

Hospitals are not the only previous land use to watch out for. You also need to be careful about land on which there used to be an execution ground, abattoir, police station or anything else that connotes death, suffering and pain. Such places are also more prone to being haunted, and even if they are not, you should definitely arrange for some kind of purification ceremony to get rid of these inauspicious and harmful energies. The Chinese usually invite their monks and lamas to bless the energies of the home and I know that my Catholic and Christian friends also invite their pastor or priest to bless their new homes. Whether you want to do something like this is entirely a personal decision.

Newly built homes carry the left-over energies of the land and its historical environment while old houses carry the energies of their previous owners. When you tune into the soul of a home it is these antiquated energies that you will probably be picking up. If the previous family had a happy, auspicious tenure in the home, the chances are that the energies left over will be positive, and vice versa.

This of its own accord does not, however, guarantee that your feng shui will be good or bad. All this does is give you a feel for the energies that used to be there. Getting the feel alone is insufficient for improving the feng shui of any place. But it helps. Homes that possess extremely sad or extremely happy energies are easy to feel, to identify and to deal with. It is the large store of in-between moods that are more difficult to get a handle on. It is simply an imbalance of energies, and these can be corrected with little effort.

Choosing a new house

When house hunting, try to do it in the mornings or in any case before the sun goes down. You should never go house hunting in the evenings and at night. This creates inauspicious energy which then attaches to your house search. Feng shui masters are generally quite particular about this rule. Those who are authentic usually prefer to visit homes and sites during the early morning hours, just after sunrise. In fact, feng shui masters of the old school will never undertake a feng shui site consultation after noon. Some even refuse to go out on an inauspicious day.

Those who are less strict (or more commercial) with themselves will continue through the afternoons but rarely do they proceed with their site investigations with the Luo Pan open after the sun goes down. This causes them to receive inauspicious feng shui. Those who wish to make feng shui consulting their profession should learn about these special taboos to protect their own feng shui.

When you start to tune into the soul of a home you will realize that the mood strongly reflects the energies of the residents. Thus the effect of good feng shui always multiplies itself since homes that are occupied by winners who are successful and happy will always be happy homes. This positive energy, in turn, attracts additional joyful energies that bring good fortune. But auspicious energies can be adversely affected.

Changing skylines and new buildings, roads and other man-made structures all affect the feng shui of your home – often in a negative way. Thus a large building or simply a house built directly in front of you will surely block your luck and you will have to do something about it.

New roads also cause havoc to the feng shui of the neighbourhood, as do new shopping malls, factories, warehouses, depots and urban redevelopment projects. You must acquire mindfulness towards the changes in your immediate environment and make adjustments where necessary to safeguard your auspicious orientations and arrangements.

The feng shui of your home can also be affected by trees that become so awesome they overwhelm you. This is a very real problem in tropical countries where plants and trees grow so fast. You must trim and cut and control the trees and plants that grow in your environment. Do not allow the sun to be blocked out completely. This is when yin energy begins to stagnate and accumulate, leading to grave misfortunes and illnesses.

Develop an affinity with sunlight, which is the source of much good fortune. It is the best natural source of yang energy. When you see the sun coming in to your home you will feel your spirits rise because the sun brings the vital cosmic breath. Make it a point to observe how growing trees create increasing shade that blocks out the sunlight.

Remember that when your plants stop flowering it is because they have inadequate sunshine. Their feng shui has been adversely affected, just like yours.

Changing feng shui

Feng shui can also be adversely altered by nothing other than the simple passage of time. Thus your home could have been giving you excellent and auspicious luck for as long as twenty years, and then suddenly everything seems to go wrong. Loss of job, loss of incomes, children getting sick, a death in the family – all happening close together. If this is your experience and your own consciousness tells you something is not quite right, you might want to check out the time dimension feng shui of your home through flying star feng shui.

Although it is an advanced branch of feng shui and outside the scope of this book, if you have done everything possible to physically enhance your feng shui and still things go wrong, you may suspect that flying stars are striking at you. In other words, use flying star feng shui as a last resort to investigate the inauspicious corners of your home at any period. If you are unfamiliar with the flying stars and you suspect this might be the cause, simply move your furniture around and see if you feel a difference. If you do, then it is likely that the location of your important furniture (beds, desks or dining tables) might have been in places where adverse flying stars have flown in.

As a habit, I change the arrangement of my furniture at least once every 18 months to create new flows to the energy patterns in my home. This always stimulates the good cosmic chi. It is also a good way of making sure energies do not stagnate and turn inauspicious. Each time I move my furniture around, I identify at least one piece of old furniture, a painting or a decorative object that I want to give away, and then I replace it with new objects. In fact, it is often a new acquisition that is the catalyst for me to move furniture around. I feel that adding something new always refreshes the energy of a room, and by extension, the home.

It is this habit that convinced me there are thousands of ways of arranging and mixing pieces of furniture, shapes and objects in a room and still have good feng shui. I discovered that as long as I stayed guided by the fundamentals of this ancient science and did not try to deviate from basic guidelines, I would continue to enjoy good feng shui. I also discovered that in applying these principles one could be as imaginative and as creative as one wished. In short, as long as the soul of the home stays fundamentally auspicious, good fortune chi continues to flow.

Feeling the harmony of spatial arrangements

Perhaps the most vital piece of the feng shui jigsaw is the way the energy flows in any given room. When spatial harmony exists, the drift of energy will be slow and circuitous and therefore auspicious. The energy moves effortlessly from room to room and from corner to corner. The elements of each corner blend amicably with each other. There are no jarring notes and no clash of energies.

When this kind of flow is attained, the home enjoys an abundance of the good feeling. There is an air of relaxed goodwill in the ambience of the home. Shouting at each other is non-existent, and every member of the household is nice and civil to each other. This level of excellence in feng shui is not easy to achieve but it is what you should aim for.

To start with, the rooms must not be over furnished and over decorated. There should be a feeling of space and spaciousness and room for people to move about comfortably. Corners and sharp edges should be non-existent and ceilings at a respectable height, neither too high nor too low. Look for pretty cornices with no pointed extremities and camouflage overhead and structural beams and columns with thoughtful design. Ensure curtains do not smother the room with either their texture or their colour and place plants in moderate quantities. Paintings should blend with the mood rather than create discordant notes.

In arranging furniture, try not to let the pieces jut out and create sharp edges. Instead, let the furniture fit nicely into the walls. Custom-made, built-in furniture is always better feng shui than single pieces standing in the middle of the room. In the living rooms, choose symmetrical arrangements that form a square or rectangle and avoid L-shaped or U-shaped arrangements. Definitely avoid asymmetrical arrangements and designs. These are inauspicious.

Single level floors are always better feng shui than multi- or split levels. Mezzanine floors seldom represent good feng shui since they divide the flow of energy.

Staircases

Staircases should always be designed with care. Try to have a staircase on one side of the home rather than in the centre. Curved staircases are good for the flow of chi but spiral staircases cause real problems (see page 135). If there are more than two levels in your home it is better not to have a continuous staircase all the way to the top floor, especially when they are curved or circular. When staircases going up and going down are located next to each other, the flow of energy becomes seriously impaired. When staircases like this directly face the main door, good fortune chi entering the home becomes confused whether to flow up or down.

In your spatial arrangements it is vital to ensure that the movement of human traffic, and therefore the flow of chi, is made to meander. The house has to be designed in a way that doors and doorways are not placed in one straight line. This layout feature causes the traffic to move whoosh in a straight line. This is a deadly flow of energy. Place some kind of divider – a screen or a row of plants or some decorative object – to block the straight-line flow. For example, when you have three doors in a row, placing a divider in front of the second door causes the flow to move around the obstacle. This instantly restores the feng shui of the space.

It is also a good idea to ensure that flows do not have to take 90-degree turns. Such sharp turns are as harmful as the straight line. They should be rounded rather than angular. The same is true for all arrangements. If you can observe some of these basic ground rules of feng shui you will find it easier to proceed towards energizing for all the other types of abundance. The good feng shui of one room or corner also flows gently and auspiciously to another.

Flowing with auspicious energies

With the spatial arrangements in place and the drift of energies established inside the home, the air of gentleness and happiness that pervade the space will influence members of the household in a positive way. It will be easy for them to go with the flow and be carried along a life of prosperity and well-being.

Tempers will not be frayed. Any difficulties and problems brought home from work or the office, will lose their draining effect. Family members become more patient and loving and the whole ambience is one of feeling good. The home then becomes a haven and this good feeling will help you to sail through any problem or difficulty you might then encounter that is caused by bad feng shui in your place of work.

Many people have told me they feel very relaxed and happy each time they come to my home. Mine is not a particularly smart or elaborately designed house. It is typically middle class, but it contains many different feng shui activators and energizers and there are many good fortune symbols on display. Feng shui is, after all, my lifelong passion. Maybe my visitors feel good because of these feng shui features.

Perhaps it is my fish pond that lies on the left-hand side of both my front doors. I have two doors to accommodate my husband's auspicious directions and mine. My pond is filled with happy, healthy, fat and colourful Japanese carps. The sound of water flowing is both relaxing and soothing. The fish swimming actively and the water filter working 24 hours a day creates a never-ending supply of yang energy.

Maybe it is my beautiful plants. I love my garden and lavish a great deal of time on my many varieties of orchids and tropical plants. The tropical weather allows me to bring the outdoors into my home and it is easy for me to soften every edge and corner of my home with lush greenery. The wood element also brings in growth symbolism.

Perhaps it is the picture windows in my living rooms for I have worked hard to ensure that every window looks out to beautifully landscaped grounds and plants. My windows are also non-threatening and low. They let in a great deal of natural light and on sunny days when the sun shines too bright, strategically placed cut crystal balls break up the sunshine and create stunning rainbows inside the house. My man-made rainbows truly are a sight to behold.

Maybe it is the way I have used mirrors in the dining room to create a feeling of height and space. My house looks bigger than it really is thereby creating a non-threatening spatial feel. The dining room mirror brings in the outdoors, reflecting my flower beds and doubling the food on my table at the same time.

Perhaps it is my exquisite feng shui designed glass-etched table tops with their auspicious fish motifs. Everyone who sits at my table is soothed and charmed by my glass arrowana and carp. They tell me it looks like Lalique crystal but that would be too expensive. Swimming on the glass table top are three tiny little pewter goldfish to suggest extreme good fortune for the three members of my family – my husband, our daughter and me. The family that eats together and enjoys eating together creates a happy ambience in the home. The dining room is also located in the centre of my home and is the focal point of the flow. How can I not have good feng shui?

And so, I think, it is all of the above and more. These and other feng shui features of my home are linked by an invisible flow of energy that glides slowly and gracefully throughout. I have described the effect of the flow rather than tell you exactly how each feature is connected to the next. Thus you can use your own interpretation of the meandering flow. You can design your own good feng shui currents inside your home according to the dimensions and layout constraints of your space. Do not expect this to be an easy exercise. Almost every house layout will present you with a challenge.

For every recommendation you pick up in a feng shui book, there will be something in your personal space that makes it hard for you to use. It is necessary to be ingenious about your practice so try to adapt the tips and pointers you pick up in this book. Do not kid yourself that you can use every single piece of advice. It is not possible and it is also not necessary. In feng shui if you get just one major thing correct – like the flow of energy in your home – you will enjoy tremendous good fortune.

Dissolving inauspicious and stagnant breath

To create a completely feel-good home, you will also need to continuously identify the nooks and corners of your home where stagnant chi accumulates. The most common places are the areas with the least traffic: dark corners, cupboards, storerooms. These are places where energy can become stale, tired or unhealthy.

Stagnant breath must be cleared. Dark cupboard corners must be aired, cleaned and even be given a coat of paint. Storerooms should be given an airing. All entrances and exits as well as windows should be opened regularly to let the air and the sunshine in. This will cause the rooms to be replenished with fresh and vibrant new energy from outside. If your part of the city or country is polluted, the energy that comes in will, of course, not be as good, but it is better than living with stale air and stagnant chi.

Offices and rooms that live on recycled air-conditioned energy can be veritable storerooms of stagnant energy. Such places have to be aired at least once a month.

Special techniques

There are special techniques for purifying the energies within a home but these special methods lie outside the scope of this book. It is useful to know, however, that the Chinese practice of feng shui always involves airing the home of stale energies.

In addition, we use specially-made fragrant incense to purify the doors and windows of the home. This incense must be made of herbs and grass taken from the high mountains where the energy is pure and clean. The higher the mountains where these herbs are grown, the better. In China during ancient times, the old books refer to secretly formulated incense made from legendary mountain paradise places where Gods and holy men dwelt. In my home I use specially formulated incense made specially for me from herbs grown in the Solu Khumbo region, one of the most holy parts of the Himalayan mountain range.

Dark corners of the home where energies stagnate can be completely purified with the magic of sounds made by specially-made bells and other objects. In addition, certain cleansing mantras can also be chanted when clearing the space of stale and bad energies.

Symbolic feel-good stimulants

The most easily available feel-good stimulants to place in the home are wind chimes, plants and crystal. Placed correctly, these objects create wonderful feelings of well-being. I have already given guidelines and advice on the use of these feng shui stimulants. It is a good idea to use them in your public rooms – your living and dining areas – so that you see them each day when you return home.

Displaying art that brings bliss

If you wish to feel happy, optimistic and energetic in your home, it is important not to hang paintings (or prints) of wizened old men or women. No matter how well painted and how much character you see in the face, pictures of men or women with weather beaten, sad faces are simply not good feng shui.

I am appalled that there are actually people who hang distorted ugly faces in their homes. There is a painting by Picasso called *Weeping Woman* in which the suggestion of sorrow, despair and sadness come across so well I want to run a mile from the painting. Yet I have seen a print in at least three homes. Needless to say, those were not happy homes. In all three instances, the marriage broke up, causing extreme distress to the wife.

Paintings of fierce animals also attract hostile energy. Tigers, lions, leopards, panthers and so forth should have no place in the home. They are wild, threatening and angry and the energies they create cause danger to the house.

Instead, the best paintings are of landscapes. Wealthy Chinese homes were always decorated with beautiful paintings of mountains with waterfalls and rivers. These landscape paintings have feng shui significance since they are usually hung strategically to provide support for the family. Paintings of mountains, for example, are always hung behind the patriarch's ornate chair so that the patriarch is always adequately supported.

Likewise, paintings of good fortune symbols such as fruits and flowers feature prominently among subjects you might want to consider for your home. The peach is very popular because it is a symbol of extreme robust health leading to a very long life. The peony is a symbol of marriage and love.

The third category of good luck paintings is religious paintings. Pictures of deities and words from the Bible, the Koran or other holy books are regarded as holy objects which bring very precious blessings to the home. No matter what religion you belong to, if you bring religious paintings into your living space and you treat them with respect, they create wonderful feel-good feng shui for the home.

In my home, the walls are hung with exquisite thangkas – Buddhist religious paintings of Buddhas – and I have no doubt at all that it is these paintings that create the air and ambience of serenity which so many visitors to my home notice. In addition to religious art, many faiths also have their own prayers or mantras. These work like good fortune symbols and if you have them, I strongly recommend their presence in your home.

Dedications that seal in good fortune

When you create good feng shui in your home, do so with good motivation. Try to produce good feng shui for yourself without harming the feng shui of your neighbour. Try not to use hostile objects to hit at the house across the road. Instead, use plants to camouflage, and a concave mirror to absorb harmful features.

Then, when you have done with making all the feng shui changes to your home make a silent dedication that you are creating good feng shui to benefit every member of your family, and every member of your neighbourhood. Follow this by listing all the aspirations and all the different types of good luck you have been creating for each member of the family. Verbalizing your aspirations in this way seals in the good feng shui of your house. Do this mental summing up each time you introduce changes to the home.

Meet Lillian Too . . .
whose credentials speak for her

Lillian Too was the first woman in Asia to become the Chief Executive Officer of a Bank – the Grindlays Dao Heng Bank in Hong Kong. In Malaysia, where she comes from, Lillian Too is described by *Malaysian Business*, the country's leading business magazine as, '. . . something of a legend in corporate circles being the first woman there to become the Managing Director of a publicly listed company.'

Lillian is an MBA graduate from the Harvard Business School, in Boston USA. She has also been described as being 'in a league of her own' by one of the country's leading magazines: *Success*. The internationally acclaimed *Vogue* magazine describes her 'as someone people listen to'.

Lillian was not simply a successful corporate woman. As a business lady she also made enough money never to have to work again. In the early Nineties, she retired from working life to become a full-time mother. That was when she started a new career in writing. To date she has penned 21 bestsellers, 19 of which are on her favourite subject of feng shui, which she says was greatly responsible for giving her masses of luck during her corporate career days, and in her business dealings. Her feng shui books have been translated into 15 languages.

In 1997, the phenomenal worldwide success of her internationally published book *The Complete Illustrated Guide to Feng Shui* made waves in the non-fictional book trade. Released in October 1996, the book has made the bestseller lists of various countries, including the UK's Times Bookwatch list. It also became the number one bestseller over the summer of 1997 in the Barnes and Noble bestseller list of the United States.

Her latest achievement has been the successful launch of her *Feng Shui Kit*, as well as her series of *Feng Shui Fundamentals* – nine little books advising how to use feng shui in nine easy lessons, and how to use feng shui for love, wealth, career, health, children, networking, fame and education. In the spring of 1998, Rider books, an imprint of Random House, published *Feng Shui Essentials* with considerable success. Lillian Too is married and has one daughter.

The Maitreya Project

LILLIAN TOO is also an Executive Director of Maitreya Project International, which is the organization that is building what will be the world's largest Buddha statue of the future Buddha Maitreya in Bodhgaya in India. Lillian enjoys devoting time and enthusiasm to this wonderful project. She says: 'Those of us fortunate enough to be working on the Maitreya project under the spiritual guidance of the most venerable and precious Lama Zopa Rinpoche have realized from the start the enormity of the task facing us. Often the sheer size and scope of what we are involved in has overwhelmed us. But it has been an increasingly uplifting and inspiring experience.

'I want to share the excitement and joy of participating in this wonderful Dharma project. The building of a holy object as large as this, and in such a revered holy place as Bodhgaya in India where the Buddha Shakyamuni gained Enlightenment, brings such inconceivable merit and will benefit so many future generations of people spiritually, that its successful completion, hopefully in the year 2008, will require much help, support and the active involvement of thousands of people.

'We need help. We need expertise. We need people with time and commitment. Presently we are at the stage where we are finalizing the development of the prototype, using cutting-edge computer and scanning technology from the United States to simulate a variety of weather conditions and to identify the best materials to use, and the best way to build the statue, thereby ensuring it will last a thousand years.

'When completed, Maitreya Buddha will tower 150 metres above the blue skies of Bodhgaya. This will be three times the statue of Liberty. Around it will be a complex of parklands and monasteries.

There will be a school and a hospital to serve the people of the surrounding regions, this being one of the poorest places in the world. Most of all, Maitreya will be a shining symbol of loving kindness for the new millennium.'

If you would like to know more about the project, we invite you to visit the Maitreya website at:

www.maitreya-statue.org

Lillian Too's website

Welcome to Lillian Too's world of feng shui on the worldwide web. Visit her website at www.lillian-too.com and e-mail her if you need clarification on any aspect of feng shui practice. Her e-mail address for readers of this book is abundance@lillian-too.com. Lillian also has a new website to explore at www.worldoffengshui.com with news about latest feng shui developments and book reviews.

Index

Acknowledgements

I want to thank the designer of my book cover – it is a splendidly original way of depicting a frolicking dragon made happy with abundance. I have placed it on my computer as a screen saver to bring me good luck! You can do the same. I want to thank Judith Kendra for encouraging me to develop my ideas for this very special book and I want to thank my Editor and Designer for pulling the book together so well without losing anything of its essence.